SCA

Sexual Violence Against Girls in South African Schools

Human Rights Watch
New York • Washington • London • Brussels

Copyright © March 2001 by Human Rights Watch.
All rights reserved.
Printed in the United States of America

ISBN: 1564322572
Library of Congress Control Number: 2001087292

Cover photo: Copyright © 1999 Nadine Hutton
Cover photo of schoolgirls at an assembly in Mpumalanga, South Africa
Cover design by Rafael Jiménez

Addresses for Human Rights Watch
350 Fifth Avenue, 34th Floor, New York, NY 10118-3299
Tel: (212) 290-4700, Fax: (212) 736-1300, E-mail: hrwnyc@hrw.org

1630 Connecticut Avenue, N.W., Suite 500, Washington, DC 20009
Tel: (202) 612-4321, Fax: (202) 612-4333, E-mail: hrwdc@hrw.org

33 Islington High Street, N1 9LH London, UK
Tel: (171) 713-1995, Fax: (171) 713-1800, E-mail: hrwatchuk@gn.apc.org

15 Rue Van Campenhout, 1000 Brussels, Belgium
Tel: (2) 732-2009, Fax: (2) 732-0471, E-mail:hrwatcheu@skynet.be

Web Site Address: http://www.hrw.org

Listserv address: To subscribe to the list, send an e-mail message to majordomo@igc.apc.org with "subscribe hrw-news" in the body of the message (leave the subject line blank).

Human Rights Watch is dedicated to
protecting the human rights of people around the world.

We stand with victims and activists to prevent
discrimination, to uphold political freedom, to protect people from inhumane
conduct in wartime, and to bring offenders to justice.

We investigate and expose
human rights violations and hold abusers accountable.

We challenge governments and those who hold power to end abusive practices
and respect international human rights law.

We enlist the public and the international
community to support the cause of human rights for all.

HUMAN RIGHTS WATCH

Human Rights Watch conducts regular, systematic investigations of human rights abuses in some seventy countries around the world. Our reputation for timely, reliable disclosures has made us an essential source of information for those concerned with human rights. We address the human rights practices of governments of all political stripes, of all geopolitical alignments, and of all ethnic and religious persuasions. Human Rights Watch defends freedom of thought and expression, due process and equal protection of the law, and a vigorous civil society; we document and denounce murders, disappearances, torture, arbitrary imprisonment, discrimination, and other abuses of internationally recognized human rights. Our goal is to hold governments accountable if they transgress the rights of their people.

Human Rights Watch began in 1978 with the founding of its Europe and Central Asia division (then known as Helsinki Watch). Today, it also includes divisions covering Africa, the Americas, Asia, and the Middle East. In addition, it includes three thematic divisions on arms, children's rights, and women's rights. It maintains offices in New York, Washington, Los Angeles, London, Brussels, Moscow, Dushanbe, and Bangkok. Human Rights Watch is an independent, nongovernmental organization, supported by contributions from private individuals and foundations worldwide. It accepts no government funds, directly or indirectly.

The staff includes Kenneth Roth, executive director; Michele Alexander, development director; Reed Brody, advocacy director; Carroll Bogert, communications director; Barbara Guglielmo, finance director; Jeri Laber special advisor; Lotte Leicht, Brussels office director; Michael McClintock, deputy program director; Patrick Minges, publications director; Maria Pignataro Nielsen, human resources director; Jemera Rone, counsel; Malcolm Smart, program director; Wilder Tayler, general counsel; and Joanna Weschler, United Nations representative. Jonathan Fanton is the chair of the board. Robert L. Bernstein is the founding chair.

The regional directors of Human Rights Watch are Peter Takirambudde, Africa; José Miguel Vivanco, Americas; Sidney Jones, Asia; Holly Cartner, Europe and Central Asia; and Hanny Megally, Middle East and North Africa. The thematic division directors are Joost R. Hiltermann, arms; Lois Whitman, children's; and Regan Ralph, women's.

The members of the board of directors are Jonathan Fanton, chair; Lisa Anderson, Robert L. Bernstein, David M. Brown, William Carmichael, Dorothy Cullman, Gina Despres, Irene Diamond, Adrian W. DeWind, Fiona Druckenmiller, Edith Everett, Michael E. Gellert, Vartan Gregorian, Alice H. Henkin, James F. Hoge, Stephen L. Kass, Marina Pinto Kaufman, Bruce Klatsky, Joanne Leedom-Ackerman, Josh Mailman, Yolanda T. Moses, Samuel K. Murumba, Andrew Nathan, Jane Olson, Peter Osnos, Kathleen Peratis, Bruce Rabb, Sigrid Rausing, Orville Schell, Sid Sheinberg, Gary G. Sick, Malcolm Smith, Domna Stanton, John J. Studzinski, and Maya Wiley. Robert L. Bernstein is the founding chair of Human Rights Watch.

TABLE OF CONTENTS

I. PREFACE 1
II. SUMMARY 4
    Sexual Violence in South African Schools 5
    Effects on Education 6
    Response and Redress 6
    South Africa's Obligations Under International and National Law 8
    Methodology 9
III. RECOMMENDATIONS 11
    To the Government of South Africa: 11
        Protection from Perpetrators of Abuse 12
        Abuse Prevention 14
        Victim Support and Protection 14
        Children and the Justice System 15
        Investigation and Documentation of Abuse 15
    To the South African Council of Educators and the Teachers' Unions of South Africa: 15
    To Teachers' Training Colleges: 16
    To the International Community: 16
IV. BACKGROUND 18
    Impact of the Political, Social, and Economic Environment on Education ... 18
    School Violence and Apartheid Era Education 18
    Sexual Violence in South African Society 20
    Sexual Violence Against Girls 23
    Attitudes Towards Violence Against Women 27
    School Reform, Conditions, and Structure 28
    HIV/AIDS and Education 32
    Schools as Spaces for Violence 32
V. SEXUAL VIOLENCE IN SCHOOLS 36
    Rape and Sexual Coercion By Teachers and School Employees 36
        The Case of MC 37
        The Case of SF 40
    Sexual Abuse, Advances, and Harassment by Teachers 42
    Abusing Authority to Take Advantage of Vulnerability 44
    "Dating" Relationships 47
    Rape and Sexual Violence By Students 48
        The Case of LB 49
    Sexual Assault and Intimidation 51
    Dating, Relationship, and Retaliation Violence 54
    Sexual Harassment 56

Violence in Transit to and from School 59
VI. CONSEQUENCES OF GENDER VIOLENCE FOR GIRLS'
EDUCATION AND HEALTH 61
    Impact on Girls' Education... 61
        Education Interrupted.. 61
        Diminished School Performance 63
        Emotional and Behavioral Impact... 64
    Impact on Girls' Health 66
        Unwanted Pregnancy and Pregnancy Discrimination 66
        Risk of Sexually Transmitted Infections... 68
VII. THE SCHOOL RESPONSE 71
    Barriers to Reporting Abuse 71
    Indifferent or Inadequate Response 74
    Ostracizing and Marginalizing Victims 76
    Lack of Procedures and Ignorance of Existing Policy 77
    Fear of Getting Involved.. 79
    Shielding Perpetrators and Concealing Abuse.. 80
    Failure to Cooperate with Investigators 84
    Inappropriate Responses.. 86
    Supporting Victims of Violence 86
VIII. THE CRIMINAL JUSTICE SYSTEM 88
    Reform Efforts... 88
    Response of the Criminal Justice System to Gender Violence in Schools 90
IX. NATIONAL AND PROVINCIAL GOVERNMENT RESPONSE 93
    Legal Reforms 95
    Guidelines on HIV/AIDS 96
    National Initiatives on School Violence 97
    National Initiatives on Gender Equity 98
    Provincial Initiatives.. 100
    Initiatives of Professional Associations 101
    Nongovernmental Partnership Projects... 101
    Challenges Ahead 103
        Identification and Tracking of Abusive Teachers 103
        Reporting Mechanisms 104
        Protection for Complainants 104
        Coordination and Communication of Policies 105
X. SOUTH AFRICA'S OBLIGATIONS UNDER INTERNATIONAL AND
NATIONAL LAW 106
    International Law... 106
        Sexual Violence as Discrimination 106
        The Right to Nondiscriminatory Education 108
    National Law 110

XI. CONCLUSION	112
ACKNOWLEDGEMENTS	113
APPENDICES	114
Appendix A:	114
Appendix B:	124
Appendix C:	132
Appendix D:	134

I. PREFACE

[E]ducation is the single most vital element in combating poverty, empowering women, protecting children from hazardous and exploitative labor and sexual exploitation, promoting human rights and democracy, protecting the environment and influencing population growth. Education is a path towards international peace and security.

Kofi A. Annan, Secretary-General of the United Nations

Education is recognized internationally as a fundamental human right—but according to the United Nations Children's Fund 130 million children of school age in the developing world, 21 percent of all school-age children, had no access to basic education in 1998. Nearly two-thirds of the children who are denied their right to education are female. Appropriately, the international community has identified girls' education as a critical priority.

Discrimination against girls based on gender perpetuates the educational gap between boys and girls. While much attention has been directed to barriers girls face in getting to school, the obstacles girls encounter at school also merit serious consideration—gender-based violence chief among them. Policy makers must place emphasis not only on getting girls to school, but also on keeping them there by keeping them safe at school. Ensuring children's equal access to education is not enough.

On a daily basis in schools across the nation, South African girls of every race and economic class encounter sexual violence and harassment at school that impedes their realization of the right to education. This report examines the barrier to equal educational opportunity posed by the South African government's failure to adequately address the gender violence prevalent in the South African school system. South Africa was selected for this study not only because of the scope of the problem but also because of the opportunities for change there, where educators both in and outside of government have shown increasing interest in finding solutions.

Emphasizing the importance of girls' education as "an effective social development policy with immediate benefits for health and nutrition as well as long term potential for preventing conflict and building peace," United Nations Secretary-General Kofi Annan launched a ten-year initiative on girl's education at the opening of the World Education Forum in Dakar, Senegal on April 26, 2000. Organized and convened jointly by the United Nations Development Fund (UNDP), the United Nations Educational, Scientific and Cultural

Organization (UNESCO), the United Nations Population Fund (UNFPA), the United Nations Children's Fund (UNICEF), and the World Bank, the World Education Forum brought together heads of state, education ministers, and representatives from more than one hundred international and grassroots nongovernmental organizations.

Forum participants adopted the Dakar Framework for Action and pledged to ensure that all children, with special emphasis on girls, have access to and complete a quality basic education by 2015. The Dakar Framework for Action identifies girls in South Asia and sub-Saharan Africa as requiring particular attention if the goal is to be reached. Participating countries committed to prepare comprehensive National Education for All Plans by 2002 detailing how the goals set forth in the Dakar Framework are to be implemented.

Ten years ago, governments gathered in Jomtien, Thailand at the 1990 World Conference on Education for All and made similar promises to meet the basic learning needs of children—promises that have been broken. In 1990, South Africa was engaged in the negotiations to end minority rule and did not participate. In 2000, South Africa not only participated in the Dakar Conference, but along with other governments pledged to ensure all South African children access to education. If governments are to close the gender gap which they have identified as an urgent priority, they must confront sexual violence and harassment of girls in schools.

Gender bias keeps many girls from ever seeing the inside of a school. In many countries, girls do not have equal access to education because traditional customs and practices relegate them to subordinate status. Work and time consuming chores, early marriage, pregnancy, and poverty also keep girls out of school. Economic constraints and cultural practices may direct parental choices to favor sending their sons to school and not their daughters. The gender gap is greatest in South Asia, sub-Saharan Africa, and the Middle East. Girls from South Asia and sub-Saharan Africa comprise the majority of children with no access to basic education.

Not only are girls a majority of out-of-school children, women comprise a sizable majority of illiterate adults. More than 60 percent of the estimated 880 million illiterate adults are women. The consequences of female illiteracy are far reaching and have a direct impact on women's capacity to sustain and protect themselves and their families. The long-term social benefits of girls' education include: increased family incomes; later marriages and reduced fertility rates; reduced infant and maternal mortality rates; better nourished and healthier children and families; greater opportunities and life choices for women; better chances to avoid disease; greater political participation; and improved economic opportunities. The positive effects of education for girls accrue to the whole of society.

I. Preface

Education is lauded by world leaders as a key solution to the social ills plaguing many nations and a means to gender equality, but school environments present a major problem that has not received sufficient scrutiny. Many girls who surmount the numerous barriers that block access to school meet discriminatory treatment once at school. Girls are required to provide cleaning and maintenance services for the school, while teachers and boys use the time for academic work or leisure. Girls are made to sit at the back of classrooms. Girls' self confidence may be further eroded by teaching materials that portray women and girls as inferior.

Tolerance of gender-based violence in schools is a serious form of discriminatory treatment that compromises the learning environment and educational opportunities for girls. Girls are disproportionately the victims of physical and sexual abuse at school. Girls are raped, sexually assaulted, abused, and sexually harassed by their male classmates and even by their teachers. In South Africa, some girls have left school entirely as a result of their experiences with sexual violence.

Schools should be safe havens for learning. Education of children presents a unique opportunity to instill tolerance and respect for human rights, including gender equality. Unfortunately, too many schools are not safe and girl children are at high risk. When governments tolerate violence in school environments, children learn lessons that legitimate violence and reinforce gender inequality.

A central contention of this report is that sex discrimination in South African schools, as manifested by inadequate state response to sexual violence and harassment, impedes a girl's access to her internationally recognized human right to education on equal terms with her male classmates. Many of the problems faced by the current government in responding to violence in schools are not of its own making, yet they are none the less urgent. Human Rights Watch believes that educational institutions cannot fulfill their mission of strengthening respect for human rights when the basic bodily integrity of female students is not respected. Leadership at every level is vital to create an education system free of gender bias and sexual violence. This exploration of the situation in South African schools has relevance for schools in other countries around the world.

II. SUMMARY

I left [school] because I was raped by two guys in my class who were supposedly my friends.

WH, age thirteen, gang-raped by classmates

I didn't go back to school for one month after I came forward. Everything reminds me, wearing my school uniform reminds me of what happened. I have dreams. He [the teacher] is in my dreams. He is in the classroom laughing at me. I can hear him laughing at me in my dreams. I sometimes have to pass down the hall where his classroom was. I thought I could see him, still there. I was scared he'll still be there.

PC, age fifteen, sexually assaulted by teacher at school

All the touching at school, in class, in the corridors, all day everyday bothers me. Boys touch your bum, your breasts. Some teachers will tell the boys to stop and they may get a warning or detention, but it doesn't work. Other teachers just ignore it. You won't finish your work because they are pestering you the whole time.

MC, age fourteen, sexually harassed at school

I can't understand how nobody saw anything or helped my child. The school has caretakers, where were they? I don't feel she is safe at school.

Mother of LB, a nine-year-old girl gang-raped at school by older classmates

South African girls too often encounter violence in their schools. South African girls continue to be raped, sexually abused, sexually harassed, and assaulted at school by male classmates and teachers. For many South African girls, violence and abuse are an inevitable part of the school environment. Although girls in South Africa have better access to school than many of their counterparts in other sub-Saharan African states, they are confronted with levels of sexual violence and sexual harassment in schools that impede their access to education on equal terms with male students.

II. Summary

Violence against women in South African society generally is widely recognized to have reached levels among the highest in the world. In response, both the South African government and women's rights organizations are working to improve the state response to domestic and sexual violence. The government has also recognized that violent crime, a major social issue in South Africa, poses a threat to school safety, and education policy makers maintain that they are committed to ending sexual violence in schools. Currently, a draft policy on gender violence is close to completion and under review in at least one of South Africa's nine provinces. Nevertheless, sexual violence and harassment often go unchallenged and today constitute a significant hurdle to equal opportunity for South African girls. A more proactive, coordinated, and system-wide response is urgently needed. Ending sexual violence and harassment in South African schools will require national leadership and commitment at every level within the education system.

This report documents school-based sexual violence; reviews school and state responses to sexual violence; explains the discriminatory impact on girls' education rights when the government does not respond adequately and effectively to gender-based violence; and sets forth recommendations to rectify these problems. Because it often remains unchallenged, much of the behavior that is violent, harassing, degrading, and sexual in nature has become so normalized in many schools that it should be seen as a systemic problem for education, not merely a series of individual incidents. Proactive and preventive measures such as human rights education programs within schools, clearly articulated and enforced policies, and better coordination between the education and justice systems, are needed to combat sexual violence and create an educational environment that respects the rights of girls.

Sexual Violence in South African Schools

Human Rights Watch found that sexual abuse and harassment of girls by both teachers and other students is widespread in South Africa. In each of the three provinces visited, we documented cases of rape, assault, and sexual harassment of girls committed by both teachers and male students. Girls who encountered sexual violence at school were raped in school toilets, in empty classrooms and hallways, and in hostels and dormitories. Girls were also fondled, subjected to aggressive sexual advances, and verbally degraded at school. We found that girls from all levels of society and among all ethnic groups are affected by sexual violence at school.

Schools have long been violent places for South African children. South Africa has only recently emerged from a history in which violence was routinely used by the state as a means of exerting power. Years of violent enforcement of apartheid era policies have fueled a culture of violence. This historical legacy presents a challenge for the government as violence remains high in many areas and schools are still ill-equipped to curb violence. Violence is often sexualized, with devastating consequences for women and girls who disproportionately bear the brunt of sexual violence, not only in society at large but in schools as well.

Effects on Education

Sexual violence and harassment in South African schools erect a discriminatory barrier for young women and girls seeking an education. As a result, the government's failure to protect girl children and respond effectively to violence violates not only their bodily integrity but also their right to education.

Human Rights Watch found that sexual violence has a profoundly destabilizing effect on the education of girl children. All the rape survivors Human Rights Watch interviewed reported that their school performance suffered. All of the girls told us it was harder to concentrate on their work after their assaults. Some girls reported losing interest in school altogether, many girls transferred to new schools, others simply left school entirely.

Social workers and therapists working with girls who were raped by teachers or classmates reported, among other problems, that the girls were failing their higher education matriculation exams and losing interest in other outside activities, such as sports. Parents told Human Rights Watch that their children had become depressed, disruptive, and anxious. Teachers expressed concern that girls they knew to have experienced sexual violence at school or at the hands of their teachers or classmates were not performing up to full potential.

Response and Redress

Although some schools try hard to respond to the problem of violence, too often school officials have concealed sexual violence and delayed disciplinary action against perpetrators of such violence at great cost to victims. Rather than receiving redress from school officials, girls who do report abuse are often further victimized and stigmatized by teachers and students. Rarely do school authorities take steps to ensure that girls have a sense of security and comfort at school or to counsel and discipline boys who commit acts of violence. Many girls leave school altogether, because they feel unsafe and are unwilling to remain in an environment that has failed to protect them.

Many girls suffer the effects of sexual violence in silence, having learned submission as a survival skill. Their attackers continue to act with impunity, in part because no one takes responsibility for the problem. Human Rights Watch found a great deal of confusion over responsibility for resolving problems and

II. Summary

repeatedly encountered breaks in the chain of communication between school officials, police, and prosecutors, with all actors shifting responsibility and sexually abused girls getting lost in the shuffle.

Some school officials told Human Rights Watch that they could not take independent disciplinary measures in their school unless the victim brought formal criminal charges. In other cases, where the victim had gone to the police, schools claimed they could not take action against the accused until the courts had convicted him of the crime. School officials told Human Rights Watch they could not do anything because many victims did not press their claims; but, at the same time, many schools refused to support girls who did come forward. We found great dissatisfaction among female students, parents of victims, and teachers who brought their problems to the attention of school administrators. There is a clear need for standardized national guidelines on how to respond to such cases.

Schools prefer to deal with sexual abuse problems internally. Police, prosecutors, and social workers complained to Human Rights Watch that schools officials generally were not helpful in efforts to bring perpetrators to justice or to aid the victims of sexual violence. Often children are not believed and they are not supported when they come forward with allegations. Many girls we interviewed reported meeting with hostility from school administrators and ridicule from other students. Often, teachers who have abused pupils are free to move to new schools and prey on new victims after being accused of rape or assault at previous schools. Similarly, boys are rarely disciplined within the school.

Recently, the government has introduced initiatives designed to address crime and violence in the school environment. Corporal punishment has been declared illegal in South Africa and the National Department of Education has recently developed an instruction manual for teachers on alternative modes of discipline. The Secretariat for Safety and Security, a civilian body that advises the minister responsible for police, in cooperation with the Department of Education has developed a National Crime Prevention Strategy for schools. The legislature has amended the Employment of Educators Act to require dismissal of teachers found guilty of serious misconduct, including sexual assault of students.

South Africa has yet to implement a national policy on how to deal with the problem of sexual violence and harassment in schools. Currently, the Western Cape Province is working to introduce guidelines on gender violence in area schools. Although there are teachers' union rules and legislation prohibiting sexual relations between teachers and students, school officials seem to be at a loss as to what to do when rules are violated. The response to sexual violence and harassment committed by students is even less clear.

Human Rights Watch acknowledges both that the South African government has made significant efforts to address issues surrounding violence against women and girls, especially within the criminal justice system, and that the challenges faced are enormous and to a great extent not of its own making. The patterns of abuse discussed in this report do indicate, however, that more government action is needed, in particular at the level of schools—an area that has received less attention. By documenting these patterns, we hope to contribute constructively to the process of policy development and implementation.

We believe the problem of sexual violence in South Africa's schools is sufficiently serious to require the development of a national plan of action to address the multiple issues involved. Human Rights Watch urges the National Department of Education to develop and widely disseminate standard procedural guidelines governing how schools are to address allegations of sexual violence and harassment, specifically detailing how schools should treat victims of violence and those who are alleged to have committed such acts. While safeguarding the due process rights of all parties involved, schools must ensure that appropriate and immediate disciplinary action is taken against persons found to have violated the policy, including counseling, probation, suspension, or termination. Schools must also foster a climate of gender equality, in order to advance mutual respect between boys and girls and prevent future student abuses.

South Africa's Obligations Under International and National Law

International human rights law requires states to address persistent violations of human rights and take measures to prevent their occurrence. With respect to violations of bodily integrity, states have a duty to prosecute whether a government official or a private citizen perpetrates the abuse. The International Covenant on Civil and Political Rights (ICCPR), which South Africa ratified on December 10, 1998, requires the government to ensure the rights to life and security of the person of all individuals in its jurisdiction. Similarly, the South African constitution enshrines the right to bodily and psychological integrity and the right to life, and recognizes the inherent dignity of all human beings and the right to have that dignity respected and protected. In compliance with international and national law, South Africa must take all appropriate steps to prevent state agents and private actors from committing acts of violence against girls in South African schools.

The Convention on the Elimination of All Forms of Discrimination Against Women (CEDAW), which South Africa ratified on December 15, 1995,

II. Summary

requires the government to take action to eliminate violence against women as a form of discrimination that inhibits women's ability to enjoy rights and freedoms on a basis of equality with men. South Africa's CEDAW obligations also extend to the provision of an effective remedy to victims of violence. Similarly, the South African constitution prohibits unfair discrimination against anyone directly or indirectly on the ground of gender, sex, or pregnancy, among other things. South Africa is obliged by its ratification of international treaties and enactment of domestic laws to ensure respect for women's and girls' human rights and fundamental freedoms, including the right to education.

International human rights law and South African law guarantee children the right to education and forbid discrimination in the realization of that right. South Africa is party to the Convention on the Rights of the Child, which recognizes the right of children to education and requires the government to provide education on the basis of equal opportunity. Similarly, the South African Constitution guarantees the right to a basic education, including adult basic education and further education, which the state, through reasonable measures, must make progressively available and accessible. In South Africa, state failure to address the problems of rape, sexual abuse, and sexual harassment of girls at school has a discriminatory impact and effectively denies girls their right to education.

Methodology

In March and April 2000, Human Rights Watch investigated cases of alleged rape, sexual abuse, and harassment involving schoolgirls in South Africa, and the government's response to gender violence in schools. Human Rights Watch researchers worked with South African nongovernmental organizations that receive hundreds of reports of school-based sexual violence each year, investigating some of these cases and documenting twenty-three incidents of girls who were raped at school. Our researchers visited eight public schools in three provinces and conducted detailed interviews with thirty-six girls about their experiences with sexual violence and sexual harassment. Girls were interviewed individually and in small groups, and all girls were interviewed outside the presence of teachers or government officials. At every school we visited, we also interviewed teachers and school administrators about sexual violence and the school's response to abuse allegations made by girls we interviewed. We conducted interviews in KwaZulu-Natal, Gauteng, and the Western Cape provinces, predominantly in urban area schools; some schools served wealthier students and others were in impoverished communities.

Independent of our school visits, Human Rights Watch also interviewed girls who had been victims of sexual abuse and sexual harassment at school but were no longer attending school. Where parents preferred that we not interview children who had been raped at school, who in many instances were still highly traumatized or under treatment, we received testimonies from the children's parents and social workers familiar with the cases. Victims in the cases we investigated ranged in age from seven to seventeen. In this report, the names of all children interviewed have been changed and substituted with initials to protect their privacy. The initials used do not correlate to the actual names of any children interviewed.

We also spoke with many of the girls' parents and teachers as well as social workers and therapists treating girls for trauma. In the course of the investigation, we met with human rights lawyers and activists, journalists, police officials, prosecutors, judges, teachers, and provincial education department officials. We also interviewed several high-ranking government officials, including the Senior Superintendent Commander of the Family Violence, Child Protection and Sexual Offences Unit of the South African Police Service and the Special Director of the Sexual Offence and Community Affairs Unit of the Office of the National Director of Public Prosecutions. Our findings are based largely on these interviews and visits to schools.

Data collected by South African groups is consistent with our findings. This includes documentation of cases reported to the telephone hotline of Childline, a social service agency working with victims of child abuse that assisted in the conduct of this study.[1] This information confirmed the general findings of our own interviews with girls and makes clear the urgency of the problem of school-based sexual violence against girls. In what follows, we draw on both our own interviews and the data of South African groups.

---

[1] Childline is a nonprofit, nongovernmental organization with several branches throughout South Africa. Childline was founded in Durban in 1986 and began as an informal telephone counseling services for abused children and their families. Childline now offers a wide variety of services, including telephone and face-to-face counseling, school talks, and training.

III. RECOMMENDATIONS

Human Rights Watch makes the following recommendations to the South African government relating to the education system and its response to sexual violence against girls. In addition to these specific recommendations, the recommendations included in two prior reports on violence against women are of further relevance: the recommendations made in *Violence Against Women in South Africa: The State Response to Domestic Violence and Rape* (1995), and *South Africa: Violence Against Women and the Medico-Legal System* (1997) are included in the appendix to this report.[2] Some of the measures proposed in prior recommendations as well as those set out below have already been adopted or are being considered by the national and some provincial governments; others have received less attention.

It is of primary importance that the National Department of Education provide leadership and mobilize commitment for combating sexual violence in schools at every level in the education system.

To the Government of South Africa:
To ensure a more effective response to sexual violence against girls in schools, the national Department of Education should:

- Adopt a National Plan of Action on Sexual Violence and Harassment in Schools

    A plan of action should be developed in wide consultation with all stakeholders, including representatives of pupils, teachers, principals, parents, social workers, government officials responsible for gender issues, NGOs offering support and advocacy services to victims, and others. It should include at a minimum, where not already in place:

    - Guidelines to schools detailing the appropriate response to allegations by pupils of rape, sexual assault, or harassment, whether by teachers or fellow pupils, including sections relating to the creation of accessible school procedures by which pupils can make confidential complaints, the prompt and effective investigation of such complaints, prompt and appropriate disciplinary action including due process protections for the persons alleged to have perpetrated the offense,

---

[2] The general recommendations set forth in prior Human Rights Watch reports on violence against women in South Africa are included in Appendix A.

referral to the criminal justice system, the report of sexual misconduct cases to the provincial department of education, and support services;

- Appropriate procedures governing the consequences for teachers or pupils who have been convicted on criminal charges of sexual violence, or who have been found after an administrative hearing procedure complying with due process protections to have engaged in sexual misconduct;

- A provision for funding of counseling and medical services for victims of sexual violence;

- A code of conduct for teachers and pupils that expressly prohibits sexual violence, harassment, and other sexual misconduct in schools. The code of conduct should be distributed to all schools and its contents widely publicized among those in the education system. Teachers should be obliged to follow the code of conduct as part of their employment contract;

- A provision for compulsory education and training for pupils, teachers, and principals on issues related to sexual violence and harassment and gender discrimination, including methods for the early identification of, and intervention to prevent, abusive behavior;

- The formal appointment in every provincial education department of a director responsible for implementing policy on gender-based violence in schools, with appropriate authority and a sufficient budget;

- Mechanisms to hold schools accountable for failure to adequately respond to allegations of sexual violence through school-based administrative measures or for failure to cooperate with investigations conducted by the criminal justice system.

In addition, the following steps should be considered:

Protection from Perpetrators of Abuse

- Laws that make failure to report child abuse to relevant authorities a criminal offense should be widely publicized and enforced, and all school employees should be educated about their obligations to report child abuse to the relevant authorities.

III. Recommendations

- Laws (including the amendments to the 1998 Employment of Educators Act introduced in 2000) that require dismissal of educators found guilty of serious misconduct including committing an act of sexual assault against a student, having a sexual relationship with a student of the school where he or she is employed, and seriously assaulting a student with the intention to cause grievous bodily harm, should be widely publicized among school principals and enforced.

- Teachers facing allegations of sexual misconduct should at a minimum be separated during classroom time from the complaining pupils. Teachers should receive notice of allegations against them as well as an opportunity to be heard by disciplinary structures. Teachers facing allegations of rape or sexual assault should be suspended with pay, the allegations reported to the police, and the suspension continued pending police investigation and trial, or the outcome of a disciplinary hearing if the case does not proceed to trial.

- Individuals who have been convicted of sexual assault or rape should not be permitted to teach anywhere in the South African school system. Before the employment of any teacher, schools should review teachers' records for incidents of sexual abuse, including inquiring with prior employers and police. School principals should be required to report confirmed incidents of sexual misconduct by teachers to provincial departments of education, which information should be maintained in a confidential database that should be checked prior to a school hiring any teacher.

- Pupils facing allegations of sexual assault or rape should receive guidance and counseling and should face disciplinary action if the allegations are sustained. Disciplinary action should have rehabilitation as a central aim and should ensure that children are dealt with in a manner that is appropriate to their well-being, proportionate both to their circumstances and the offense, and consistent with their right to education. Appropriate disciplinary action may take a variety of forms, including reprimand and warning, supervision within the school, transfer to a different classroom, and the use of home or alternative schooling. Suspension or expulsion should be a measure of last resort when another pupil is in serious physical danger.

- In accordance with section 9 of the 1996 South African Schools Act, provincial departments of education should issue notices in the provincial government gazettes specifying the behavior by pupils which may constitute serious misconduct justifying expulsion, and the disciplinary procedures to be followed in such cases. The national Department of Education should work with provincial departments to develop these guidelines on a uniform basis, ensure that sexual abuse is addressed within them, and disseminate them widely among school principals and other relevant stakeholders.

- Because girls often do not have the same access to interdicts or formal orders of protection as women, the creation of a school-based interdict or restraining order to be enforced on school grounds by school employees to protect the victim's safety should be considered.

Abuse Prevention

- School governing bodies should be required to address the problem of sexual violence and its prevention as a regular agenda item, and special meetings should be held to address specific cases. Every governing body should designate a member, preferably female, whom pupils, parents, or teachers concerned about sexual abuse can approach for assistance and who is responsible for ensuring that policies on sexual abuse are followed. Training should be made available to these individuals by provincial departments of education.

- Schools should foster collaboration with relevant NGOs working on rape, sexual assault, child abuse, or domestic violence issues, for the purposes of providing training, counseling, and advocacy services.

Victim Support and Protection

- Provincial departments of education and health should take steps to ensure that the health care and psychological needs of victims of sexual assault are met and that victims receive appropriate treatment for associated injuries, infections, and related trauma. This should include the provision to victims of medical assistance consistent with the prevailing best practice on post Human Immunodeficiency Virus/Acquired Immunodeficiency Syndrome (HIV/AIDS) exposure prophylaxis and to all pupils and teachers of current, culturally appropriate, and clear information on HIV/AIDS.

III. Recommendations

- Provincial departments of education should take steps to prevent the practice of virginity testing in schools and should develop educational materials to address the issues surrounding this practice.

Children and the Justice System

Children in the justice system are entitled to a fair hearing and the equal protection of the law, in accordance with international standards. If accused of infringing the law, children have the right to treatment in a manner consistent with the promotion of their sense of dignity and worth, taking into account their age and the desirability of promoting their reintegration into society.

- In accordance with current government efforts to improve the justice system and provide support to victims, children required to give evidence in court should receive pre-trial legal counseling and be adequately prepared for trial, and have access to intermediaries who can translate court proceedings into "child-friendly language," and to facilities to enable them to give testimony outside the presence of the accused.

- Pupils should be informed of their rights within the justice system. The national and provincial education departments should develop mechanisms for coordination with and improved access to schools by officials of the criminal justice system, including police, prosecutors, or social workers, and for officials who face problems in carrying out their work in schools to have recourse to authorities within the education department to ensure a school's cooperation.

Investigation and Documentation of Abuse

- In order to inform the development of effective responses to sexual violence in schools, steps should be taken to improve the collection of data concerning crimes of violence against pupils, whether by schools, provincial education departments, the police, or other appropriate bodies such as Stats SA, the government statistical service.

To the South African Council of Educators and the Teachers' Unions of South Africa:
To further efforts to end sexual violence against pupils in schools, teachers' organization should:

- Deny membership to convicted sex offenders;

- Cooperate with provincial departments of education to devise an awareness and advocacy campaign to combat sexual violence and harassment in schools in line with the National Plan of Action;

- Revoke the licenses of teachers found guilty by an administrative or criminal tribunal of serious misconduct, including the rape, sexual assault, or physical abuse of a student.

To Teachers' Training Colleges:
To prevent sexual violence and better equip teachers to respond to the problem of gender violence in schools, teachers' training colleges should:

- Increase instruction of future teachers on gender equity, including lessons on the harms of sexual violence and harassment in the school environment as a discriminatory impediment to education, and develop ways to intervene to stop sexual harassment before it escalates to violence;

- Develop in-service training programs for experienced teachers on the prevention of, and response to, sexual violence and harassment in their schools. Offer these workshops throughout the country. Appoint a faculty member within each teacher training college to coordinate training and research efforts;

- Educate teachers on their responsibilities under any code of conduct that is developed.

To the International Community:
To ensure high standards of response to sexual violence against girls in schools the international community should:

- Provide technical support and funding for programs to train South African teachers in gender equity and strategies for preventing sexual violence and harassment in the school environment. Support programs that educate teachers, parents, and society at large about the harm of sexual violence and harassment to girl children and their education;

III. Recommendations

- Mobilize strong national and international support for school-based human rights education programs to teach students about their human rights, including the right to be free from violence on grounds of gender, and the rights enshrined in the Convention on the Rights of the Child;

- Fund governmental and nongovernmental organizations providing direct medical, counseling, and support services to women and children who have been victims of violence and sexual assault in South Africa;

- Fund initiatives to provide clear, current, accessible, and culturally appropriate information on HIV/AIDS transmission and the basics of AIDS as a disease in the curriculum of primary and secondary schools, in teacher training, and in the training of school administrators;

- Fund efforts to provide medical assistance consistent with the prevailing post HIV/AIDS exposure prophylaxis to decrease the likelihood of contracting the virus for victims of sexual violence;

- Encourage South Africa and other nations that pledged at the Dakar World Education for All Forum to develop or strengthen National Education for All Action Plans to detail strategies for addressing school-based gender violence in their National Action Plans;

- The U.N. Committee on the Rights of the Child should inquire into sexual violence and harassment in schools and encourage countries to make efforts to address school-based gender violence. The U.N. Special Rapporteur on the Right to Education should investigate the problem of gender-based violence in schools and its impact on children and the right to education. U.N. agencies, including UNICEF and UNESCO, should support programs that teach educators and students about gender equality, the rights of the child, and human rights;

IV. BACKGROUND

Impact of the Political, Social, and Economic Environment on Education

The sexual violence South African girls encounter in their schools takes place against the backdrop of a violent South African society. State-sponsored violence used to maintain order was a constant feature of the apartheid regime. The apartheid regime has left a legacy of social and economic inequality. Extremely high levels of violence persist throughout South African society, to which women and girls are not immune. Indeed, women and girls are often most vulnerable, particularly to various forms of gender-based violence—violence that is either directed against women and girls because they are female, or violence that affects women and girls disproportionately.

The South African education system, although engaged in meaningful reform measures, faces severe problems in overcoming the legacy of the past in the face of limited fiscal resources in the present day. An education system so weakened is susceptible to any number of social ills—among them gender violence.[3]

School Violence and Apartheid Era Education

The political, social, and economic conditions of South Africa have been shaped and devastated by apartheid. The heavy burden this violent legacy places on schools makes it all the more critical that school authorities intervene to stop violence in schools and create safe learning environments for students.[4]

The South African education system today is still scarred by the racially discriminatory policies of apartheid, and in particular the system of "Bantu Education" imposed by the National Party government. Until the transition to democracy in 1994, the apartheid regime brutally enforced racially

---

[3] In this report the terms gender violence and sexual violence are used interchangeably and refer to any physical violence that is directed against women and girls because they are female or violence that affects females disproportionately such as rape, sexual assault, sexual abuse, and indecent assault.

Rape is defined consistent with current South African law as unlawful sexual intercourse with a female without her consent. Statutory rape is sexual intercourse with a girl under the age of sixteen.

Sexual assault is used to describe violence or unwanted physical contact of a sexual nature that does not meet the South African legal definition of rape, including but not limited to oral and anal penetration, sexual penetration with objects, and attempted rape.

Sexual harassment is used to refer to unwanted sexual advances whether or not accompanied by physical contact and unsolicited sexualized degrading language. Sexual abuse or gender abuse will be used generally to describe all of the above.

[4] In this report "student" is used interchangeably with "learners" and "pupils" to describe children under the age of eighteen years attending school.

IV. Background

discriminatory social policies designed to promote and preserve white domination. During the period of resistance against apartheid schools were transformed into sites of political struggle and frequently became violent spaces.[5]

Apartheid was formally applied to education in South Africa with enactment of the Bantu Education Act in 1953,[6] which required that apartheid education be geared to meet white demand for semi-skilled labor.[7] Accordingly, funding for education was also allocated on an unequal basis. Schools attended by blacks were grossly under-funded and understaffed.[8]

---

[5] There is a large literature on the political history of education in South Africa. See, generally, Jonathan Hyslop, *Classroom Struggle: Policy and Resistance in South Africa 1940-1990* (Durban: University of Natal Press, 1999); Pam Christie, *The Right to Learn: The Struggle for Education in South Africa* (Johannesburg: Ravan Press, 1985); Neville Alexander, *Education and the Struggle for National Liberation in South Africa* (Trenton: Africa World Press, 1992); Simphiwe Hlatshwayo, *Education and Independence: Education in South Africa, 1658-1988* (Westport: Greenwood Publishing Group, 1999); Peter Kallaway (ed.), *Apartheid and Education: The Education of Black South Africans* (Johannesburg: Ravan Press, 1984); John Marcum (ed.), *Education, Race and Social Change in South Africa* (Berkeley: University of California Press, 1982).

[6] Educational segregation based on race in South Africa originated before the advent of apartheid, when Dutch and British settlers founded separate schools for their slaves to teach rudimentary language skills in order to facilitate basic communication. The Cape School Board Act 35 of 1905 was the first official law mandating separate education according to race, paving the way for a long history of separate education for blacks and whites in South Africa. See Andrew van Zyl, "A Historical Overview of South African Education," in E.M. Lemmer and D.C. Badenhorst (eds.), *Education for South African Teachers* (Pretoria: Juta and Co., 1997), pp. 54-55.

[7] "Bantu education" policies were designed to ensure that the vast majority of black children would receive a schooling that did not equip them for anything other than unskilled manual labor, while white children were prepared for an almost complete monopoly of the dominant positions in the society. African girls studied subjects designed to prepare them for jobs as domestic servants. The intention of securing white domination through education was apparent in the National Party's justification for the Bantu Education Act. National Party Minister of Native Affairs (and later Prime Minister) Dr. H.F. Verwoerd maintained:

> There is no place for him [the black person] in the European community above the level of certain forms of labour....Until now he has been subject to a school system which drew him away from his own community and misled him by showing him the green pastures of European society in which he will not be allowed to graze.

See F. Troup, *Forbidden Pastures: Education Under Apartheid* (London: International Defence and Aid Fund, 1976), p. 22.

[8] *Education for All: The South African Assessment Report 2000* (Pretoria: Department of Education, March 2000), p. 5.

The government's insistence on the use of Afrikaans as a medium of instruction brought the student resistance movement to a head, culminating in the student demonstrations of 1976 that began in Soweto.[9] Already the site of conflict, schools became the locus of increasing violence as the education crisis intensified and student expectations were frustrated.[10]

Today, school violence poses a fundamental challenge to the government as it confronts the formidable task of dismantling apartheid and inculcating a "culture of learning" among youth who remain disillusioned and marginalized.[11] Children's exposure to violence, combined with heightened levels of frustration and increased aggression, have given rise to novel problems within the education system, compromising the culture of learning.[12]

Sexual Violence in South African Society

The sexual violence that has infiltrated South African schools is prevalent in South African society at large. Human Rights Watch has previously investigated this problem in two reports: *Violence Against Women in South Africa: State Response to Domestic Violence and Rape* (1995), and *South Africa: Violence Against Women and the Medico-Legal System* (1997). Since our prior reports, the number of reported rapes in South Africa has risen dramatically, due perhaps both to increased reporting and to an actual increase in violence against women. The reported incidence of rape and attempted rape

---

[9]Soweto is an acronym derived from South-Western Townships. Soweto is the largest black township in South Africa and is located just southwest of Johannesburg. For discussions on student movements in South Africa, see Jonathan Hyslop, "Schools, Unemployment, and Youth: Origins and Significance of Student and Youth Movements," in Bill Nasson and John Samuel (eds.), *Education: From Poverty to Liberty* (Johannesburg: David Philip Publishers, 1990).
[10]Rueben Mogano, *The Resurgence of Pupil Power: Explaining Violence in African Schools*, Seminar Paper presented at the Centre for the Study of Violence and Reconciliation, March 24, 1993, Seminar No. 1 (Johannesburg: Centre for the Study of Violence and Reconciliation, 1993), available at http://wits.ac.za/csvr/papmogan.htm (accessed December 10, 1999).
[11]Ibid., pp. 1-2
[12]Ibid., p. 7. For further discussions of the challenges confronting educational reform in South Africa, see, generally, Shireen Motala, Salim Vally and Maropen Modiba (eds.), "A Call to Action: A Review of Minister K. Asmal's Educational Priorities," *Quarterly Review of Education and Training in South Africa*, vol. 6, no. 3, 1999; Peter Kallaway, *Education After Apartheid: South African Education in Transition* (Cape Town: UCT Press, 1997); Zandile Nkabinde, *An Analysis of Educational Challenges in the New South Africa* (Lanham: University Press of America, 1997).

IV. Background

increased by 20 percent from 1994 to 1999—though there are serious concerns about the quality of the statistics.[13]

South Africa reportedly has one of the highest rates of violence against women in the world.[14] A 1996 comparison of South African crime ratios to those in over one hundred other countries revealed South Africa to be the leader in the incidence of murder, rape, robbery, and violent theft.[15] In 1998, three out of ten women surveyed in the Southern Metropolitan region of Johannesburg reported that they had been victims of sexual violence in the previous year.[16] Seventy-seven percent of women described sexual violence as "very common" in their areas. Sixty-eight percent of women said they had been subjected to some form of sexual harassment at work or school at some point in their lives.[17] One in four young men questioned reported having had sex with a woman without her consent by the time he had reached eighteen.[18]

According to the most recently available South African Police Service statistics, there were 51,249 cases of rape reported to police nationally in 1999.[19]

---

[13] South African Police Service, "Semester Report 1/2000, Annexure A: National and Provincial Crime Statistics: January – December: 1994-1999," in *The Incidence of Serious Crime in South Africa Between January and December 1999* (Pretoria: Crime Information Analyis Centre, Crime Intelligence, South African Police Service, 2000), available at http://www.saps.co.za (accessed November 28, 2000).

[14] Internationally, all crimes including rape are reported as incidence statistics for a given year. Statistics on incidence of rape are reported in ratios per 100,000 of the population. South Africa's distinction as a world leader in rape is largely based on a comparison of selected crime ratios from South Africa for the year 1996 with the crime ratios from 113 other Interpol member countries, as reported in *International Crime Statistics* (Interpol, 1996).

[15] South African Police Service, "Semester Report 1/1999, Annexure E: International Crime Ratios According to the 1996 Interpol Report," in *The Incidence of Serious Crime in South Africa Between January and December 1998* (Pretoria: Crime Information Analysis Centre, Crime Intelligence, South African Police Service, 1999), available at http://www.saps.co.za (accessed November 28, 2000).

[16] Alan Martin, "Horror that Stalks Women Everywhere," *Sowetan*, August 24, 1998.

[17] Neil Andersson, Sharmila Mhatre, Nzwakie Mqotsi, and Marina Penderis, *Prevention of Sexual Violence: A Social Audit of the Role of the Police in the Jurisdiction of Johannesburg's Southern Metropolitan Local Council* (CIETafrica: Johannesburg 1998), p. 10.

[18] Cornia Pretorius, "One in Four Men Say They are Rapists," *Sunday Times*, June 25, 2000.

[19] South African Police Service, "Annexure A: National and Provincial Crime Statistics: January – December: 1994 – 1999," *The Incidence of Serious Crime in South Africa Between January and December 1999* (Pretoria: Crime Information Analysis Centre,

According to the South African police, rape continues to be one of the most under-reported crimes, and therefore unpunished.[20] Rape ranks last on the list of South African crimes in terms of conviction rates.[21] A considerable percentage of cases are withdrawn before they reach court or during court proceedings.[22] There is a significant backlog of cases in the justice system with some rape cases taking as long as two years to be finalized.[23] Trials for child victims regularly take longer than trials with adult victims and witnesses.[24]

The prevalence of rape and violence against women in South Africa remains highly contested. President Thabo Mbeki has criticized the country's rape statistics as inflated and "purely speculative."[25] South African women's rights groups counter that the magnitude of the problem cannot be reflected solely in statistics and warn against creating a debate centered around the accuracy of numbers.[26] At this writing, Minister of Safety and Security Steve Tshwete and National Police Commissioner Jackie Selebi have ordered a moratorium on the release of government crime statistics on the ground that compilation of the statistics requires reassessment.[27]

Crime intelligence, South African Police Service, 2000); Glenda Daniles, "Getting Women to Report Rape," *Mail and Guardian*, August 4, 2000.

[20] See Human Rights Watch, *Violence Against Women in South Africa: State Response to Domestic Violence and Rape* (New York: Human Rights Watch, 1995), pp. 50-51.

[21] Ros Hirschowitz, Seble Worku, and Mark Orkin, *Quantitative Research Findings on Rape in South Africa* (Pretoria: Statistics South Africa, 2000), pp. 21-24. Only one out of eleven (8.9 percent) of all reported rape cases end up in the conviction of the perpetrator whereas half (53.3 percent) of drunken-driving and drug related cases result in conviction. Ibid. See also Andersson, et al., *Prevention of Sexual Violence*, p. 14.

[22] Hirschowitz, et al., *Quantitative Research Findings on Rape in South Africa*, p. 24.

[23] Ibid.

[24] Human Rights Watch interview with Thoko Majokweni, Special Director Sexual Offence and Community Affairs Unit, National Prosecuting Authority of South Africa, Pretoria, March 22, 2000.

[25] Phindile Ngubane and Robert Brand, "Mbeki Slams 'Speculative' Rape Stats," *Star*, October 28, 1999.

[26] In a letter to President Mbeki endorsed by several women's rights groups, Rape Crisis Cape Town expressed concern over his rejection of frequently cited rape statistics. Available at http://www.rapecrisis.org.za/views/mbeki.html (accessed October 17, 2000).

[27] Reportedly, National Police Commissioner Jackie Selebi ordered a freeze on the release of all local crime statistics in what has been explained as an attempt to give the police time to reassess and restructure the way the department measures crime. See "Gag on Crime Stats 'Till Further Notice,'" *Mail and Guardian*, July 14, 2000; Ted Leggett, "Crime Statistics Moratorium Is No Solution," *Mail and Guardian*, August 24, 2000.

Sexual Violence Against Girls

According to a 1997 South African government report, rape and sexual abuse of children are increasing rapidly and are matters of grave concern.[28] From 1996 to 1998, girls aged seventeen and under constituted approximately 40 percent of reported rape and attempted rape victims nationally.[29] Twenty percent of young women surveyed in southern Johannesburg reported a history of sexual abuse by the age of eighteen.[30] Another recent study investigating sexual violence suggests that there has been a steady increase in the proportion of women reporting having been raped before age fifteen.[31]

According to 1998 figures from the South African Police Service (SAPS) Child Protection Unit and the Victims of Crime Survey from 1999, rape is the most prevalent reported crime against children, accounting for one-third of all serious offenses against children reported between 1996 and 1998.[32] According to a SAPS statistical analysis of reported rape cases, the victim age group reflecting the highest rape ratio per 100,000 of the female population is the category of twelve to seventeen-year-old girls, with 471.7 cases.[33] The age category of zero to eleven years of age reflected a ratio of 130.1 rapes per 100,000 of the female population.[34]

---

[28]Government of National Unity, *Initial Country Report: South Africa: Convention on the Rights of the Child* (South Africa: Government of National Unity, 1997), p. 60.
[29]Hirschowitz, et al., *Quantitative Research Findings on Rape in South Africa*, pp. 21-24.
[30]Neil Andersson, Sharmila Mhatre, Nzwakie Mqotsi, and Marina Penderis, *Beyond Victims and Villains: The Culture of Sexual Violence in South Johannesburg* (Johannesburg: CIETafrica, 2000), pp. 48-59.
[31]Human Rights Watch interview with Rachel Jewkes, Acting Director Women's Health Research Unit, Medical Research Council, Pretoria, March 20, 2000; see also Hirshowitz et al., *Quantitative Research Findings on Rape in South Africa*.
[32]See Kimberley Porteus, *Tirisano: Towards an Intervention Strategy to Address Youth Violence in Schools Working Document* (Pretoria: Secretariat for Safety and Security, the Department of Education and the National Youth Commission, 1999), p. 10, and sources cited therein.
[33]South African Police Service, "Statistical Analysis of Reported Rape Cases," in *The Incidence of Serious Crime in South Africa Between January and December 1999*. For the twelve to seventeen-year-old age group, the Western Cape reflected the highest ratio of rapes at 889.3 per 100,000 of the female population, followed by Gauteng at 722.0.
[34]Ibid. For the age category of zero to eleven years, Gauteng was identified as the province with the highest ratio of reported rape cases per 100,000 of the female population with 220.9 cases, followed by the Western Cape at 176.4, Free State at 149.4, and KwaZulu-Natal at 139.2.

Because those who commit acts of sexual violence can also be very young,[35] girls may have real reason to fear the threats and taunts of their classmates. The SAPS reportedly has seen increases in the number of children being arrested for acts of sexual violence. In Mitchell's Plain, a township community in the Western Cape, up to 40 percent of the 950 sexual violence cases recorded in 1999 were reportedly committed by children.[36] A prosecutor in Durban told Human Rights Watch: "I'm seeing many more younger and younger perpetrators—school aged kids."[37]

Some researchers attribute the increase in sexual violence against girls to a belief gaining credence in some communities that sexual intercourse with a young virgin can "cleanse" HIV-positive men or men with AIDS of the disease.[38] Justice officials in KwaZulu-Natal, for example, are concerned that

---

[35] Girls are the most frequent victims of sexual assault including rape, attempted rape, and other sexual offenses. Fear of sexual violence is very prevalent among girls. Even very young girls are aware of sexual violence and frightened of falling victim to it. One South African researcher told us of focus groups conducted among girls in Gauteng which revealed that

> girls as young as eight to twelve knew what rape was; when asked what do you like about being a girl they came up with nothing; they wanted to be boys; they were afraid of rape and boys beating them up. Bullying in schools is a big problem, if not always gender related.

Human Rights Watch interview with Sue Goldstone, Soul City, Johannesburg, March 17, 2000. Soul City is a multi-media project initiated by the Institute for Urban Primary Healthcare. It uses popular entertainment to educate the South African public on various health topics. Soul City develops television and radio programming around particular themes or areas of concern often after conducting research among its potential target audience.

[36] Janet Heard, "Young Life Shattered After Horror at School," *Sunday Times*, August 8, 1999.

[37] Human Rights Watch interview with Val Melis, Senior Public Prosecutor, Family Matters, Durban, April 3, 2000.

[38] Prega Govender, "Child Rape: A Taboo Within the AIDS Taboo," *Sunday Times*, April 4, 1999; Peter Dickson, "Myth of 'Virgin Cure' May Be Linked to Rape," *Sunday Times*, September 27, 1998. According to Suzanne Leclerc Madlala, an anthropologist at University of Durban Westville, the "virgin cure" myth is based in the belief that a man will somehow get an infusion of "clean blood" through intercourse with a virgin. Virgins are also believed to have special immunity against sexually transmitted diseases due to a dry vaginal tract. Prepubescent girls are not seen as having the same vaginal secretions of adult women. Leclerc Madlala's research found that the virgin girls were perceived as physically clean, morally clean, uncontaminated, and able to transfer these properties to others. According to Leclerc Madlala,"[the myth] is a sensitive issue with potentially racist overtones, people don't want to confront the issue."

IV. Background

the myth may be fueling an increase in child rape cases. One prosecutor told Human Rights Watch:

> The virgin rape myth is a major problem. I represent a lot of HIV-positive kids, they die. The kids often die before we are able to finish the prosecution of their abuser. We're seeing younger and younger victims with an average age of six—guaranteed to be virgins. I am seeing more than one HIV-positive child a week. I can't completely attribute all their HIV status to the virgin rape myth, because it could be that the mother was HIV-positive, but I do feel the myth is causing an increasing number of younger rape victims.[39]

Some research suggests that child rape is also committed as a preventive measure to avoid contracting the virus from older women. In part, because they are believed to be HIV-free, younger women and girls have become increasingly attractive to older men as sexual partners, willing or unwilling. Because they are commonly believed to be less likely to be infected, very young girls run an increased risk of sexual harassment on their way to and from school. Girls have been abducted and sexually assaulted in route to school. This has led to isolated cases of such girls being withdrawn from school and to pressure from parents for schools to be built closer to their homes.[40]

Human Rights Watch is concerned that the prevalence of the belief that sexual intercourse with virgins cures HIV/AIDS may pose a risk to young girls. Our interviews with child abuse activists and counselors indicate that the virgin myth is a real problem.[41]

> It is difficult to say where the myth about sex with a virgin will cure AIDS came from—some believe that it was from traditional healers. What we do know is that it causes enormous suffering to children who become the victims of this misinformation and we believe the myth should be actively targeted in the media and all HIV/AIDS education programs.[42]

---

[39] Human Rights Watch interview with Val Melis, Senior Public Prosecutor, Durban, April 3, 2000.
[40] M.J. Kelly, *The Encounter Between HIV/AIDS and Education* (Harare: UNESCO, 2000), p.18.
[41] Human Rights Watch interview with Joan van Niekerk, Director Childline, Durban, April 8, 2000.
[42] Jean Redpath, "Children at Risk," *Focus,* June 2000, pp. 23-25.

The director of Childline also believes her counselors are "certainly seeing young children who appear to have been the victims of [the myth]. They have been abused by adults and youths who are HIV-positive and ordinarily would not be sexually attracted to or active with children." The director reported: "We know of township youths who specifically target virgin girls and separate them physically from their peer groups—for instance, when walking home from school—and gang rape them."[43]

At the same time that virgins are being targeted for sexual assault, Human Rights Watch received reports that virginity tests were being conducted at some schools in KwaZulu-Natal.[44] Reportedly, at eight schools in Osizweni, local teachers administered tests to as many as 3,000 children and awarded certificates to students who passed.[45] There are accounts of children as young as six being pressured to take part in virginity testing conducted by teachers in schools in Osizweni. At some schools in the area, testing reportedly is conducted every three months.

The practice of virginity testing of girls, predominantly in KwaZulu-Natal, has been lauded as a way to delay the sexual activity of youth and prevent the spread of HIV.[46] Virginity testing as an HIV/AIDS prevention measure is

---

[43]Ibid.
[44]Prega Govender, "Schoolkids in Virginity Test," *Sunday Times*, May 17, 1998. According to B. Mohlaka:
> Virginity testing was conducted by older women who were often related to the child. Now teachers often conduct this kind of testing. Various other researchers also stated that schoolteachers conducted these examinations mainly on girls, who, should the test be passed, were awarded with virginity certificates.

B. Mohlaka, Member of Parliament, Address at the *Commission on Gender Equality Consultative Conference on Virginity Testing* (June 12, 2000).
[45]Govender, "Schoolkids in Virginity Test," *Sunday Times*. According to Futhi Zikalala of the Commission for Gender Equality: "The way these [virginity] tests are done infringe on a girl's right to privacy. Girls have to lie on their backs with their panties off and legs up in the air, preferably on a sloped floor." Human Rights Watch interview with Futhi Zikalala, Provincial Manager, Commission for Gender Equality, Durban, March 30, 2000.
[46]Ansuyah Maharaj, "Virginity Testing a Matter of Abuse or Prevention?," *Agenda*, no. 41, 1999; "South Africa: Virginity Testing," *IRIN HIV/AIDS Weekly*, Issue 8, January 5, 2001; Chris McGreal, "Virgin Tests Make a Comeback," *Mail and Guardian*, September 29, 1999; Zwelihle Memela, "Virginity Testers Fight for Their 'Cultural Rights,'" *Natal Witness*, December 6, 2000.

The practice of virginity testing is not limited to KwaZulu-Natal. According to women's rights groups, testing is increasing in prevalence. In response to the growing prevalence of virginity testing in the South Africa, the Commission on Gender Equality (CGE), the South African Human Rights Commission (SAHRC), and the National Youth Commission (NYC) hosted a consultative conference June 12 to 14, 2000. See *CGE*

overly invasive for girls. Virginity testing infringes on a girl child's right to privacy, is gender discrimination, and violates the right to bodily integrity.[47] Human Rights Watch maintains that schools are especially inappropriate sites for virginity testing. There is an implicit state endorsement when testing is conducted on school property or by school officials, and we urge an end to school testing, and encourage continued education about HIV/AIDS transmission to dispel the "virgin myth."

Attitudes Towards Violence Against Women

Societal attitudes toward women and girls also contribute to a higher incidence of violence against them.[48] According to a recent Gauteng area study, eight in ten young men believed women were responsible for causing sexual violence and three in ten thought women who were raped "asked for it." Two in

---

Consultative Conference on Virginity Testing Report. The conference brought together virginity testers and others to discuss ways of promoting gender equality by harmonizing cultural practices with constitutional provisions.

Proponents of virginity testing maintain that the practice is being revived for a variety of reasons, including: a return to Zulu (African) culture; prevention of HIV/AIDS and teenage pregnancy; promotion of morality; detection of child sexual abuse and incest; and preservation of virginity before marriage. See "Virginity Testing as Cultural Practice," *CGE Conference Report* (June 2000), pp. 20-26.

The CGE and others have objected to virginity testing on gender equality grounds. The CGE maintains that virginity testing violates the privacy of a child because it is often conduced in public in open fields or community halls. CGE has raised concerns that there is no standard training or guidelines to qualify one to become a tester, that testers use different methods, and that they do not adhere to principles of hygiene and could encourage the spread of sexually transmitted diseases. The CGE has noted that virginity testing has failed to reduce the incidence of HIV/AIDS or teenage pregnancies. See "Culture Human Rights, and Virginity Testing," *CGE Conference Report* (June 2000), pp. 32-44.

Child abuse counselors are concerned that testing may raise the threat of abuse or discrimination against girl children who fail the tests. In one case reported to Childline, a girl's relatives broke both her arms after she failed a virginity test. Human Rights Watch telephone interview with Joan van Niekerk, Childline, January 12, 2001.

[47]For additional discussion of virginity testing and violations of women's physical integrity, see Human Rights Watch, *A Matter of Power: State Control of Women's Virginity in Turkey* (New York: Human Rights Watch, 1994).

[48]Lisa Vetten, "Roots of a Rape Crisis," *Crime and Conflict*, no. 8, Summer 1997; see also Lauren Segal, Joy Pelo, and Pule Rampa, "'Asicamtheni Magnets—Let's Talk, Magents:' Youth Attitudes Towards Crime," *Crime and Conflict*, no. 15, Autumn 1999.

ten thought women enjoyed being raped.[49] Among male youth who knew a woman who had been raped, 7 percent said they thought she must have enjoyed it and 24 percent thought she "asked for it." Nearly half the males surveyed said they had sexually violent male friends. Three in ten men said they could be violent to a girl.

Nearly 50 percent of male youth said they believed a girl who said "no" to sex meant "yes." Nearly a third of both men and women surveyed said forcing sex on someone you know is not sexual violence.[50] Some girls even responded that they did not have the right not to be subjected to sexual violence.[51] While the majority of men thought "jack-rolling" ("recreational" gang rape) was "bad," young people between the ages of fifteen and nineteen years old were the most likely to say it was "good" or "just a game."[52] Eleven percent of fifteen-year-old male youth thought jack-rolling was "cool," with a leap in male opinion in favor of jack-rolling between the ages of sixteen and seventeen.[53]

Youth attitudes regarding violence against girls help perpetuate violence. To date, the education system has not been effective in changing attitudes or teaching students to control aggression; rather, schools are spaces where violence remains prevalent in part because it is not effectively challenged by school authorities.

School Reform, Conditions, and Structure

The South African government has placed great emphasis on the development of policies to redress the legacy of disparities and inequalities left by apartheid. Significant investments are being made in education.[54] The South African Schools Act of 1996[55] and the National Education Policy Act of 1996[56]

---

[49]Andersson et al, *Beyond Victims and Villains*, pp. 53-57. CIETafrica researchers interviewed youth on three separate occasions, surveying 1,471 youth in 1998, 9,555 youth in 1999, and 16,338 youth in 2000. Youth were of school age ranging from ten to eighteen years of age, attending grades 8-12, and representing twenty-five schools in Johannesburg.
[50]Ibid.
[51]Ibid.
[52]Ibid., p. 24.
[53]Ibid., p. 56.
[54]The proportion of the total budget allocated to education has remained virtually constant between 1995 and 1998, averaging 22 percent. Department of Education, *Education for All: The South African Assessment Report 2000* (Pretoria: Department of Education, March 2000), p. xii. There has been an increase in overall expenditure on education, with expenditure increasing from R34.1 billion in 1995-96 to R45.2 billion during 1998-99. Per capita expenditure on primary school education is R2,370. Ibid.
[55]The South African Schools Act, No. 84 of 1996.
[56]The National Education Policy Act, No. 27 of 1996.

govern the administration of education in South Africa. The South African Schools Act repealed the many discriminatory education laws that existed under the apartheid education system, setting forth a new and nationally uniform education system for the nondiscriminatory organization, management, and financing of schools.

Similarly, the National Education Policy Act is aimed at "the advancement and protection of the fundamental rights of every person" to education as guaranteed in the constitution.[57] The act empowers the national minister of education to determine national education policy in terms of the principles embodied in the constitution. The act provides an infrastructure that requires consultation with a wide variety of bodies before determining policy, including a body representative of the organized teaching profession, a national council of college rectors, a national council representative of students, and a national council representative of parents. The act ensures the publication and implementation of national education policy and also calls for the evaluation and monitoring of education in South Africa.

The government dismantled the pre-1994 education system, consolidating the eighteen segregated departments into one central department and nine provincial departments.[58] The former Department of National Education has become the Department of Education, which coordinates education at the national level and is mainly responsible for policy formulation and monitoring of implementation.

The constitution vests substantial powers in provincial legislatures and governments to run education affairs subject to the national policy framework, and each province also has an education department.[59] South African schools are governed by statutes enacted by the central and the provincial legislatures. Provincial statutes on education vary from province to province, but are essentially the same in that they provide a legal framework and basic legal principles for the provision, governance, and function of education.

The Council of Education Ministers (made up of the national minister of education and the provincial members of the executive councils (MECs) responsible for education), and the Heads of Education Departments Committee (made up of the top civil servants in the national and provincial departments) facilitate cooperation between the national and provincial structures to enable the departments to share information and advice and to collaborate on policy

---

[57] Ibid., Section 4.
[58] Department of Education, *Education for All Assessment,* pp.10-11.
[59] South Africa is divided into nine provinces, each with its own legislature. The 1996 constitution makes provisions for nine provinces, each with its own education department tasked with delivering education in accordance with the national education policy.

design and implementation. These structures are intended to provide a regular forum for administrative heads of education departments to consult and collaborate in the interests of the system as a whole.

School attendance is compulsory for South African children from the ages of seven to fifteen. The South African education system consists of four phases: junior and senior primary and junior and senior secondary. The junior primary phase includes the first three years of formal schooling, Grade A, Grade B, and Standard three for children aged six to eight. Standards four through six comprise senior primary for children aged nine to eleven. The primary school phase aims at developing basic skills of literacy and numeracy. The junior secondary phase, the seventh to ninth standards for children aged twelve to fourteen, bridges students from primary to secondary education with a broad-based curriculum. The senior secondary phase, the tenth to twelfth school years, prepares students aged fifteen to seventeen for the senior certificate or matriculation certificate examinations commonly known as "matric."[60]

South Africa's education system is expanding. The 1996 Schools Register of Needs study recorded 27,276 schools in the country. The number of teachers has grown from 145,000 in 1976 to 375,000 in 1996.[61] School enrollment has also grown, increasing from 10,099,214 in 1991 to 12,071,355 in 1998, representing an annual growth rate of 2.8 percent.[62]

South African's gross enrollment ratio in primary schools is 96.5 percent, though there are substantial differentials in gross enrollment by gender. The gross enrollment ratio is higher among males at 98.3 percent than among females at 86.3 percent.[63] Gross enrollment gender disparities are more pronounced in some provinces, such as Northern Province and Mpumalanga. The average student-teacher ratio in South African public primary schools is thirty-five—each teacher is responsible for an average of thirty-five students. Student-to-teacher ratios also vary substantially by province.[64]

---

[60]See E.M. Lemmer (ed.) et al., *Education for South African Teachers*, p. 152. A matriculation certificate is a prerequisite for tertiary education in South Africa.

[61] Nearly a quarter of primary school educators are deemed not appropriately qualified (either unqualified or under qualified) by the government and their employment is allowed due only to a human resource shortage, especially in rural areas. Department of Education, *Education for All Assessment*, pp. 28-29.

[62]Department of Education, *Education for All Assessment*, pp. 28-29.

[63]Ibid., p. 30. Gross enrollment measures the total number of enrollees in primary school as a percentage of the total population of primary school age children. It differs from net enrollment by including in its count older pupils as well as the number of official grade-level pupils in each grade.

[64]Ibid., p. 33. The Western Cape has the lowest student-teacher ratio and the highest budgetary allocation for primary education.

IV. Background

Sixteen percent of children six to fourteen years of age are out-of-school, though they should be attending.[65] Disparities in the proportions of out of school children vary by place of residence, population group, and gender. Proportions of out-of-school children are highest in the least developed and poorest provinces, with a non-attendance rate of 18.8 percent in the Eastern Cape, while the non-attendance rate is only 9.9 percent in the Western Cape.

Prevalence of out-of-school children also varies significantly by population group. It is highest among African children and lowest among Indians and Asians. Slightly more boys are out of school than girls. However, girls drop out of school earlier than boys, and children in rural areas tend to drop out earlier than those in urban areas.[66]

The government has acknowledged, in its assessment submitted to the World Education for All Forum 2000, that the physical environment of many schools requires urgent attention. There is still a chronic shortage of classrooms in black schools and student-teacher ratios remain unacceptably high. Most South African primary and combined schools have no access to proper sanitation facilities. Nearly half of the schools use pit latrines that are often inadequate in number and may pose health hazards; 13.5 percent of schools have no sanitation facilities at all. The majority of primary and combined schools, 56 percent, have no electricity. Five percent of primary and combined schools have buildings deemed by the government not to be suitable for education, while another 12.5 percent have buildings that need urgent attention. The condition of buildings is poorest in the Northern Province and in KwaZulu-Natal, where 41 percent and 23 percent of the schools, respectively, either need urgent attention or are not suitable for teaching and learning.[67] The government also reported that most schools lack adequate supplies of teaching and learning materials.

The general performance of South African primary school learners has been called "poor" by the government.[68] The overall pass rate for the matriculation examination has dropped from 87 percent in 1979 to 48 percent in

---

[65]Ibid., p. 35.
[66]Ibid., p. 36.
[67]Ibid., p. 37.
[68]The average score obtained by standard four students targeted in the 1999 South Africa Monitoring Learning Achievement (MLA) Survey was below 50 percent in all the tasks in which they were tested: literacy, numeracy, and life skills tasks. Department of Education, *Education for All Assessment*, p. xiv. Test scores for the year 2000 improved considerably over 1999. However, while more girls again registered for the exam, significantly fewer passed than their male peers. See Julia Grey, "Exam Results Show a Long Road Ahead," *The Teacher (Mail and Guardian)*, January 11, 2001.

1998.[69] However, the number of students taking the exam has increased 548 percent over that period, with the number of secondary school graduates rising by 267 percent.[70] Most of the students who took the 1999 matriculation examination were female, while most of those who passed were male. In each province, the pass rate was higher for males than females.[71]

HIV/AIDS and Education

In addition to the challenges associated with school reform, the education system is faced with South Africa's HIV/AIDS crisis. With a total of 4.2 million infected people, South Africa has the largest number of people living with HIV/AIDS of any country in the world.[72] The AIDS epidemic is having a massive impact in South Africa's education sector, both on the demand for and supply of education.[73]

Schools as Spaces for Violence

One of the most significant challenges to learning for many children is the threat of violence at school. South Africa's written submission to the World Education for All Forum, an assessment of the state of education in the country, identified the possession of weapons by students, sexual abuse, the use of

---

[69] "Shocking Stats on Matric Pass Rate," available at http://www.news24.co.za, January 13, 2000 (accessed February 3, 2000).

[70] According to a 2000 survey conducted by the South African Institute for Race Relations, only 6 percent of the population over the age of twenty had some form of post-matriculation education, and only 16 percent had completed grade 12. "Shocking Stats," available at http://www.news24.co.za (accessed February 3, 2000).

[71] In 1999, although females made up 55.7 percent of the 511,474 candidates in all nine provinces, the number of females who passed was only 46.1 percent, compared to 52.3 percent for males. "Gender Gap in Matric Pass Rate," available at http://www.news24.co.za, January 1, 2000 (accessed February 3, 2000). In 1996, more girls than boys took matriculation exams in each province, but proportionally fewer girls than boys passed. "Schoolboys in a Class of their Own," *Sunday Times*, January 5, 1997.

[72] Joint United Nations Programme on HIV/AIDS, *Report on the Global HIV/AIDS Epidemic* (Geneva, UNAIDS, June 2000), p. 9.

[73] According to the U.N., the HIV/AIDS epidemic is eroding the supply of teachers resulting in increased class sizes, and ultimately diminishing the quality of education. With the teacher shortage expected to worsen, researchers calculate that over 71,000 children aged six to eleven will be deprived of a primary education by the year 2005. Joint United Nations Programme on HIV/AIDS, *Report on the Global HIV/AIDS Epidemic*, p. 29. See also "HIV/AIDS in Africa: Placing it High on the Agenda of ADEA," Association for the Development of Education in Africa Newsletter, vol. 12, no. 2, April-June 2000, pp. 4-6; Charlene Smith, "SA Faces AIDS-Related Education Disaster," *Mail and Guardian*, July 26, 2000.

alcohol and drugs on school premises, and burglaries as having a debilitating effect on the morale of school managers, educators, and governing bodies.[74]

Neither the national nor provincial departments of education systematically monitor incidents of violence in schools.[75] Similarly, there are no data systems to facilitate the evaluation of crime statistics on the basis of where the crime was committed. While quantitative data on school violence is not available, the existing evidence, confirmed by Human Rights Watch's own research, strongly suggests that violence—sexual or otherwise—is prevalent in many South African schools, undermining the ability of these schools to achieve their developmental and educational objectives.[76]

School violence emanates from a variety of sources: Violence may be perpetrated by teachers, by students, and even by strangers to the school community. Teachers continue to inflict physical violence on their students in the form of corporal punishment. Although corporal punishment is illegal in South Africa,[77] many teachers still see violence as an appropriate tool for child discipline and continue to physically assault children by caning, slapping, and beating them to maintain classroom discipline, or to punish poor academic performance or improper behavior.[78]

---

[74] Department of Education, *Education for All Assessment*, p. 42. See also Corina Pretorius, "Schools Gripped by Fear," *Sunday Times*, January 31, 1999.

[75] Porteus, *Tirisano: Towards an Intervention Strategy to Address Youth Violence in Schools*, p. 6.

[76] Ibid.

[77] The South African Schools Act 84 of 1996, Section 10, prohibits the administration of corporal punishment in schools and provides for criminal sanction. See also Julia Sloth-Nielsen, "Corporal Punishment: Whipping Lobby Nears its Final Beating," *ChildrenFirst* vol. 3, no. 27, October/November, 1999. In *Christian Education SA v. Minister of Education of the Government of South Africa*, a private school challenged Section 10, asserting that the provision should be ruled unconstitutional and invalid to the extent that it prohibited the use of corporal punishment in independent or private schools. The Constitutional Court of South Africa affirmed the legality of the corporal punishment ban, concluding that whipping, whether judicially imposed or imposed in schools, is a violation of the constitutional right to be free from "all forms of violence, not to be tortured, and not to be treated or punished in a cruel, inhuman or degrading way." In *S v. Williams*, the South African Constitutional Court abolished whipping as a juvenile sentence to be imposed by courts.

[78] Reports of corporal punishment frequently appear in local press. See Matthew Burbidge, "Principal Admits Supervising Pupils Beating," *Mercury*, March 15, 2000; Craig Bishop, "Religious Teacher on Trial After Pupil Dies from Beating," *Sunday Times*, September 26, 1999. According to Childline, reports of corporal punishment in schools made to Childline increased in 2000. Human Rights Watch telephone interview with Joan van Niekerk, Childline, January 12, 2001.

High levels of racially motivated violence among students in formerly white, colored, and Indian schools that are being integrated have been reported. In a 1999 study of students in schools with high levels of racial diversity, 62 percent indicated that there had been a racial incident or racism in school, including derogatory and racial name-calling and various forms of racial harassment often resulting in physical altercations.[79]

The insecurity of the school environment presents a situation in which children are routinely exposed to gang violence, rape, robbery, and assault. Gangs operate with impunity in some school environments,[80] making "schools places where drugs, thugs and weapons can move as freely through the gates as pupils."[81] Turf wars between gang members do not just spill onto school grounds; rather, schools become territorial prizes because gangs need a controlled area from which to sell drugs and recruit members. Some schools are so destabilized by gangs that courses are not conducted according to any regular schedule. Teachers report that they sometime fear their own gang-affiliated pupils who carry weapons and smoke *dagga*.[82] Intimidation by gangs can undermine all attempts at creating a culture of learning and teaching.[83] Lack of

---

[79]Porteus, *Tirisano: Towards an Intervention Strategy to Address Youth Violence in Schools*, p. 29, citing S. Vally, Y. Dalamba, *Racism, Racial Integration, and Desegregation in South African Public Secondary Schools* (Pretoria: South African Human Rights Commission, 1999).

[80] The Independent Projects Trust (IPT), a Durban based nongovernmental organization, examined ten Durban schools during 1997 to identify the sources and conditions promoting violence and possible ways to address the problem. IPT found gang-related violence and inadequate school security were significant problems for children. Children in nine of ten schools identified gang-related violence as the "number one" problem, with the worst reports coming from Kwa Mashu and Newlands East. Children were very familiar with the existence of gangs, knew the names of gangs, and knew which boys in school were affiliated with gangs. Human Rights Watch interview with Val Smith, IPT, March 29, 2000; Richard Griggs, *Children at Risk: The Security Situation in Durban Schools* (Durban: IPT, 1997).

[81]Richard Griggs, "School Violence: A Culture of Learning About Drugs, Thugs, and Guns," *ChildrenFirst*, February/March 1998.

[82]Common slang usage for marijuana.

[83]Students in IPT focus group sessions spoke about a culture of silence; since they were the targets of gang activities, they were reluctant to reveal the severity of violence. Human Rights Watch interview with Val Smith, IPT, March 29, 2000.

IV. Background 35

school security is a problem in high crime areas.[84] In many schools, teachers and students alike are frightened for their safety.[85]

---

[84]Human Rights Watch interview with Alexandra township teacher, Johannesburg, March 27, 2000. One township teacher complained "We don't have security at our school. Thugs come right in and abduct girls as well as boys. There is no police presence. They only come if something is wrong."
[85]See student essays contained in Appendix B. In the essays, children describe in their own words their experiences with and thoughts and feelings about crime and violence in their lives and schools. Student essays were provided by the Crime Reduction in Schools Program (CRISP), a program based at the University of Natal funded primarily by the South African Department of Arts, Culture, Science and Technology Innovation Fund.

V. SEXUAL VIOLENCE IN SCHOOLS

Sometimes it feels scary.

JI, age sixteen, about the risk of sexual violence and harassment at her school.

Far from being a problem only for schools with few resources, sexual violence permeates the whole of the South African education system. Human Rights Watch interviewed girls from a variety of different social, economic, and ethnic backgrounds. In documenting their cases, Human Rights Watch learned that sexual assault occurs in prestigious predominantly white schools, in impoverished predominantly black township schools, in schools for the learning disabled, and even in primary schools. Privilege often does not protect a girl against sexual violence, while poverty may render her more vulnerable to assault.

South African girls face the threat of multiple forms of violence at school. This includes rape, sexual abuse, and sexualized touching or emotional abuse in the form of threats of violence. Girls also encounter constant highly sexualized verbal degradation in the school environment. These forms of gender violence are largely committed by other students, and in some instances by teachers or other school employees. Even strangers to the school environment target young women in schools, or on their way to and from school.

Rape and Sexual Coercion By Teachers and School Employees

There must be an end to the practice of male teachers demanding sex with schoolgirls or female teachers. It shows selfish disrespect for the rights and dignity of women and young girls. Having sex with learners betrays the trust of the community. It is also against the law. It is a disciplinary offence. Tragically, nowadays, it is spreading HIV/AIDS and bringing misery and grief to these precious young people and their families.

Kader Asmal, South Africa Education Minister[86]

---

[86]Department of Education, "Message from the Minister of Education" in *The HIV/AIDS Emergency, Guidelines for Educators* (Pretoria: Department of Education, 2000).

V. Sexual Violence in Schools

Based on our interviews with educators, social workers, children, and parents, the problem of teachers engaging in serious sexual misconduct with underage female students is widespread.[87] As the testimony offered below demonstrates, teachers have raped, sexually assaulted, and otherwise sexually abused girls. Sometimes reinforcing sexual demands with threats of physical violence or corporal punishment, teachers have sexually propositioned girls and verbally degraded them using highly sexualized language. At times, sexual relations between teachers and students did not involve an overt use of force or threats or force; rather, teachers would abuse their authority by offering better grades or money to pressure girls for sexual favors or "dating relationships."

The Case of MC

Human Rights Watch interviewed MC, a fifteen-year-old high school student in the northern suburbs of Johannesburg. MC was living on the campus of her high school when one of her teachers asked her to come to his flat, also on the school campus, after class hours. He said he needed to speak with her. MC told Human Rights Watch what happened next:

> I was walking with [a] friend and [the teacher] asked me to come to his room...I thought, he's a teacher, it'll be fine. He gave me a key so that I could get to the boy's hostel [where he lived]. I went to his dorm and walked to the lounge. He gave me a hooch [an alcoholic drink]. I was lame. I knew what was happening to me, but I couldn't move. He picked me up and took me to his room and started taking my clothes off. He took his clothes off. He's twice my size and like five times my weight, and has so many muscles. Then he penetrated me. When I came to, I got up and went to my dorm. My friend said I looked high. I went to bed. Then I just left it. I was scared to tell anyone because I was afraid no one would believe me. I had been raped before and no one believed me then.[88]

---

[87]Sexual intercourse with a girl under the age of sixteen is a statutory crime in South Africa pursuant to Section 14 of the Sexual Offences Act, No. 23 of 1957. If a girl has consented to sexual intercourse, the male involved will be guilty only of contravening Section 14 of the Act. However, a girl under the age of twelve is by law incapable of consent. Unisa, *Women and the Law*, p. 108. According to Childline, sentences for statutory rape can vary widely from one magistrate to the next and may range from incarceration to suspended sentences to fines. Human Rights Watch telephone interview with Joan van Niekerk, Durban, January 12, 2001.

[88]Human Rights Watch interview with MC, age fifteen, Johannesburg, March 18, 2000.

MC thought she would just forget about the rape, but her aggressor would not let her. Shortly after the alleged rape, the teacher persisted in pursuing MC for sex. She told Human Rights Watch: "The next day he asked me to come back. I gave him back his key and said I didn't want to have anything to do with him."[89] The teacher still did not leave her alone, as MC had hoped. The teacher tried different approaches to lure MC back to his room, once under the pretense of private language tutoring and another time with promises of better grades. MC told us: "About a week later he asked me if I would come do Afrikaans with him, and that he would give me good marks."[90]

In subsequent weeks, another classmate confided in MC that the same teacher was making sexual advances towards her and told MC of another student who claimed to be having an affair with the same teacher. MC explained, "When I heard that, it really irritated me, because we had trusted him, and he was doing the same thing to my friends. We had problems at home and things that we couldn't really talk to our parents about, and he would talk to us. We confided in him. When I heard he was doing the same things to my friends, I came out with it."[91] MC told a trusted female teacher and later her mother.

When MC's parents went to the school to complain, they were met with a hostile reception and advised by the school principal not to report the incident to police. MC described the meeting as follows.

> Me, my mum and my dad went to see the principal and told him what happened. He said he couldn't believe it, and that if it did happen, we must keep it within the school and not tell anyone: the CPU [Child Protection Unit], the board of education. It should be between himself, [the deputy head of school], and us only. My mother said no.[92]

MC's family did not heed the school's advice and brought the case to the attention of the police. Even after the case had been filed, the school did not immediately take any action, such as initiating a disciplinary proceeding. After MC's allegations became public, at least six other girls from MC's school, aged between fourteen and sixteen, came forward and complained that the same teacher had either raped them or made sexual propositions to them.[93]

---

[89]Ibid.
[90]Ibid.
[91]Ibid.
[92]Ibid.
[93]Charlene Smith, "Asmal: School Rape a National Crisis," *Mail and Guardian,* October 15, 1999.

V. Sexual Violence in Schools

Fifteen-year-old PC, another student who said she was sexually abused by the same teacher, told Human Rights Watch of her experience as follows.

> It started he would keep me after class and we would talk about whatever was bothering me. We agreed that we needed more time to talk than just for moments after class. So he sent a note home to my parents saying I needed extra help with Afrikaans. My parents and I [later] gave this note to the police [as evidence]. [94]

According to PC, when she went to his apartment, instead of talking about her problems the teacher propositioned her, asking her to start a "dating relationship," and sexually fondled her. Initially, she was confused but flattered by the teacher's attentions. This turned to betrayal and anger when she learned she was one of several girls targeted by the teacher: "When I heard about the other girls, I asked him. I said, 'What should I do if I'm called [by police]?' He said I mustn't say anything because the other girls were lying. I had all these combined emotions. He said he cared about me. He didn't."[95]

Charlene Smith, a journalist at the Johannesburg-based *Mail and Guardian* who first brought this case to the attention of Human Rights Watch, learned that the same teacher had faced similar allegations at other schools where he had previously taught.[96] Children at a primary school in Doornfontein, where he taught from 1991 to 1995, had complained about the teacher to school officials.[97] Complaints about the teacher had also previously been made to an organization assisting victims of child abuse, but police said that they could not act until a formal complaint was lodged against the teacher and the school had not done so.

MC's teacher is presently on voluntary leave from the high school while police investigate the rape allegations. He has been charged with several counts of statutory rape (sexual intercourse with a girl under age sixteen), but the case was still pending at the time of this writing.

MC left school shortly after her allegations became public because she could no longer endure the teasing from her classmates, who would call her names including "whore," "slut," and "liar."[98] According to MC, some of the

---

[94] Human Rights Watch interview with PC, age fifteen, Johannesburg, March 18, 2000.
[95] Ibid.
[96] Human Rights Watch interview with Charlene Smith, Johannesburg, March 17, 2000; Charlene Smith, "More Abuse Claims Against Rape-Accused Teacher," *Mail and Guardian*, September, 24, 1999.
[97] Ibid.
[98] Human Rights Watch interview with MC's mother, Johannesburg, March 18, 2000.

other students would taunt her, "They say 'you shagged the teacher,' but I didn't, he raped me."[99]

MC's mother explained, "It is hard for her to go to school and face that [the constant ridicule]; she doesn't want to go, she can't handle being rejected by the others. She's been in emotional upheaval, she hates school and she's fighting everyone. It has affected our entire family."[100]

MC's case was unusual primarily because she had the courage to come forward and enjoyed the support of her parents who pressed the case. However, MC's case is not atypical in that she did not find support from school officials. That MC alleged she was raped at school by a school employee, and that school officials chose to conceal the allegations within the school community, is sadly representative of what many South African girls experience. Human Rights Watch received testimony illustrating a persistent pattern of teachers implicated in serious abuses being able to continue to work within the school system.

The Case of SF

A Durban school serving learning-disabled children took no action after a teacher allegedly raped a sixteen-year-old student, SF, in 1998. On the day of the assault, SF had been asked to go the principal's office and help staple papers. When she arrived, the principal was not in the office and SF found herself alone with a male instructor who had an office adjoining the principal's office. According to SF, the teacher raped her and forced her to perform oral sex. He then threatened her with violence if she told anyone.

Later the same day, a teacher's aide approached SF during a recess period because she "looked troubled." SF disclosed the rape to the aide. Taking SF with her, the teacher's aide reported the rape to the school principal. According to the aide the school principal reportedly said "[SF] looks fine now" and that she did not believe SF's allegations. SF was returned to her classes to complete the school day and was sent home on the bus with her classmates.

Coincidentally, SF's mother had called the school principal that same day to discuss school bus issues. SF's mother believes that she called the principal after SF had reported the rape, but the principal did not mention the rape allegations or indicate that anything out of the ordinary had occurred with SF at school during the conversation.

SF's mother told Human Rights Watch:

---

[99] Charlene Smith, "Schools Exile Children to Save Face," *Mail and Guardian*, November 9, 1999.
[100] Human Rights Watch interview with MC's mother, Johannesburg, March 18, 2000.

V. Sexual Violence in Schools

> When [SF] arrived home I knew something was wrong because she did not greet me. She didn't ring to get into the gate; she was just standing there with her head down. I asked her "what's wrong" and she didn't respond. I told [SF] to go get her bath and get ready for Arabic lessons. Later that evening, [the school principal] called to tell me that SF had made some "very serious allegations at school." They should have called me, I'd have come right to the school to get her. They wanted to hush it up because he's [the teacher is] a big shot who brings in funds for the school.[101]

The school did not initiate any disciplinary proceeding against the teacher and he remained on the job.[102] Human Rights Watch has learned that a criminal case against this teacher recently resulted in his conviction. However, he has appealed the ruling and is not currently in custody. Moreover, Childline reports that he has continued to work in educational supervisory capacities close to children, by serving on a national committee on sport for disabled athletes. The teacher continued in this capacity, despite repeated objections and warnings from Childline that he poses a danger to children.

The prosecutor bringing the case against SF's teacher shared the disappointment of SF's mother with the school's response. The prosecutor explained to Human Rights Watch:

> What is most disappointing for me is you don't get support for this girl. These are people who work with disabled children; you'd think they'd be more supportive and want to get people who are a possible danger to the kids away from the kids. I was quite shocked by this. The majority of the teachers came through wanting to testify for the defense, saying that SF lies, that she's given to fantasy because she talks about wanting to marry someone on the television show "The Bold and the Beautiful." We had SF assessed by two different, separate psychologists and [Childline]. SF is fine and she's telling the truth. She is from a very conservative Muslim family. She'd had no exposure to sex and there's not enough sex on any soap opera she'd watch to account for the level of explicit detail the child was able to provide.[103]

---

[101] Human Rights Watch interview with SF's mother, Durban, March 30, 2000. Human Rights Watch did not interview SF.
[102] Human Rights Watch telephone interview with Joan van Niekerk, January 12, 2001.
[103] Human Rights Watch interview, Val Melis, Senior Public Prosecutor, Family Matters, Durban, April 3, 2000.

As a result of the incident, SF's mother made a decision to take her out of school entirely. She told Human Rights Watch, "I'm still afraid I can't keep [SF] safe."[104]

* * *

These two cases illustrate some of the abuses to which girls in South African schools are subject, including abuse of authority and violence by teachers, failure of school authorities to respond decisively to serious allegations, and, as a result, significant interruption of the girls' education. These issues surfaced repeatedly in Human Rights Watch interviews with girls and in the records of South African social services organizations assisting victims of child abuse.

Sexual Abuse, Advances, and Harassment by Teachers

A 1998 Medical Research Council survey found that among those rape victims who specified their relationship to the perpetrator, 37.7 percent said their schoolteacher or principal had raped them.[105] South African girls interviewed by Human Rights Watch reported routine sexual harassment in schools, as well as psychological coercion by teachers to engage in "dating relationships."

In some cases, girls acquiesce to sexual demands from teachers because of fears that they will be physically punished if they refuse. In other cases, teachers abuse their position of authority by promising better grades or money in exchange for sex. In the worst cases, teachers operate within a climate of seeming entitlement to sexual favors from students. In a wide spectrum of cases, the school response is weak, nonexistent, or actually facilitates continued abuse.

Human Rights Watch repeatedly encountered reports of psychological coercion. A fifteen-year-old student described how her teacher played to her emotions, sexually propositioned her, and then molested her.

---

[104]Human Rights Watch interview with SF's mother, Durban, March 30, 2000.
[105]Medical Research Council, "The South African Demographic and Health Survey of 1998," in Hirschowitz et al., *Quantitative Research Findings on Rape in South Africa* (Pretoria: Medical Research Council, 2000), pp. 16-21. Of the women surveyed, 19.8 percent said that perpetrator was a stranger or recent acquaintance, 29.6 percent said the perpetrator was a relative or someone close. The study, conducted by the Medical Research Council and the Department of Health in 1998, questioned women between fifteen and forty-nine years of age; 12,327 women responded to a survey, of those 11,735 women were interviewed. The survey covered many issues, including information on fertility, childhood mortality rates, maternal and child health, and questions devoted to violence against women.

V. Sexual Violence in Schools

He talked to me about having a dating relationship, but how it wouldn't work and how it would be wrong. Duh, I was like yeah. Then he started to give me a massage. I was kind of uncomfortable but I knew he cared about me, and he said he did a lot for his students and not all of them appreciated him. He said I was different. He said he was interested in seeing me, but it would never work because he's a teacher and I'm a student. I agreed. Then he asked me to take off my shirt but if part of my school uniform was still on I would look sexy. Then he touched me. I told him to stop. I told him it was time for my parents to come get me. My parents came ten minutes later. My whole family was in the car. My mother asked me, "How was your Afrikaans lesson?"[106]

IZ, a seventeen-year-old student from Oudtshoorn in the Western Cape, found that her teacher sexually harassed her when she sought his advice on a personal subject. IZ called Childline in August 1999 because her teacher had started to touch her and make her feel uncomfortable and she was not certain how to handle his harassment.[107]

Girls reported being subjected to degrading sexualized language from their teachers. A student told Human Rights Watch how a teacher who later raped her would make sexually explicit and degrading comments to girls in his classes about their bodies. MC described the teacher's classroom demeanor to Human Rights Watch as follows:

He would make all the girls sit in the front row, so he could look at them, and the boys in the back. He made me and my friend sit right in front of him. He would say things to us. Like one of my friends walked by and took off her blazer, and he said, "you go girl" because she has big boobs. There was a black girl in my hostel who had big boobs, and he told her she didn't need to get a boob job. You'd have to wear long pants because he would make bad comments, like "nice legs," or "can we go out." He signed my [school] diary "I love you. You go pupil."[108]

In another case reported to Childline, a primary school teacher from Chatsworth, near Durban, asked girls to draw a penis. The teacher reportedly

---

[106] Human Rights Watch interview with PC, age fifteen, Johannesburg, March 18, 1999.
[107] Childline call report, August 1999.
[108] Human Rights Watch interview with MC, age fifteen, Johannesburg, March 18, 1999.

was seen taking a girl into an empty classroom. She was then seen leaving the classroom wiping her mouth, leading the witness to believe that she had been sexually assaulted. The caller reportedly feared that the children's parents and the school governing body were not made aware of the allegations against the teacher, that no social worker was called into the school, and the "matter was simply being pushed aside."[109]

In our interviews with schoolgirls, social workers, and teachers, we encountered repeated allegations that teachers engaged in sexual relations with underage girls often without schools intervening to sanction teachers. Reports of rape and sexual abuse of girls by teachers also periodically appear in the local press. For instance, in November 2000, a middle school teacher in the North West province allegedly raped at least three underage female students, including one girl in the school library.[110]

Abusing Authority to Take Advantage of Vulnerability

Human Rights Watch documented one case in which a young girl was raped by her teacher and later paid for her silence. A social worker in KwaZulu-Natal treating the child described the case as follows:

> I have a case of a twelve-year-old girl who was having sex with her teacher in exchange for money. He raped her in an empty classroom during school. She'd left her class to go to the toilets. He gave her money for her silence. And after that she would meet him and he'd pay her. There was medical evidence of penetration. The teacher was suspended but later allowed to come back to school. He paid the girl one rand when he raped her. Another girl has said he did the same thing to her.[111]

In poorer areas abusive teachers will take advantage of a child's poverty to gain sexual access to them. A teacher familiar with the problems faced by children in poverty told Human Rights Watch:

> Usually it starts you find a teacher being very supportive, giving the child special treatment. Nobody does anything about it. The teacher will give kids money to buy food, clothes. Some parents will encourage the children to become involved with the teacher for these

---

[109] Childline call record, September 1997.
[110] Pule Waga Mabe, "Raped at School," *Mail and Guardian*, November 14, 2000.
[111] Human Rights Watch interview with Dumi Nala, Childline, Durban, March 31, 2000. In April 2000, the rate of exchange was approximately six South African rand per one U.S. dollar.

V. Sexual Violence in Schools

benefits. The teachers are taking advantage of the poverty of the children. Teachers abuse their position of respect."[112]

A provincial school official from KwaZulu-Natal found that parents of students involved in affairs with teachers often kept silent because the teacher gave them money.[113] A social worker in KwaZulu-Natal told Human Rights Watch, "Some parents don't object to affairs with teachers. They reason that 'at least he's working and has money.' 'Perhaps he'll help us support the child; take off some of the burden.' I think money plays a big role."[114] In some instances, girls reportedly initiated relationships with teachers for economic reasons. In other instances, girls who were sexually abused were paid for their silence.

Poverty and fear can also form a powerful combination making it difficult for girls to resist and complain when sexually propositioned, contributing to their vulnerability to assault. A teacher who was responsible for transporting a female student to school would make suggestive comments to her when she was alone with him in the car. The student shared her problem with a social worker, who told Human Rights Watch:

> In January, a sixteen-year-old girl came to me and told me that she had a problem. A teacher in the school, who gave her lifts to and from school, was bothering her. She lived very far away from the school, she would have to rise at 5:00 a.m. if she took public transport, and her parents had made an arrangement with the teacher, who lived near her to drive her to school in his car. There were two other kids that he drove to school with her. She started receiving lifts this year. She told me that the teacher would always drop her off last, and that he would make remarks, like "I'm tired. I need a bath. I need to be rubbed." "My wife hasn't been home. I need to be rubbed." She told him that she didn't like that kind of talk and would he stop. I advised her to tell her parents but she doesn't want to. She's afraid of him and she's dependent on him for a ride. Her parents are unemployed and the public transport fare would be too much, her sister is the only one working in the family. She was afraid

---

[112] Human Rights Watch interview with Nonhlanhla Maboa, teacher, Johannesburg, March 27, 2000.

[113] Prega Govender, "Teachers Prey on Pupils in Sex-for-Marks Scandal," *Sunday Times*, October 31, 1999.

[114] Human Rights Watch interview with Xoliswa Keke, Childline, Durban, March 29, 2000.

that her parents would approach him and take action against him, and that he would harm her. He's a big and intimidating man. You don't argue with him. He carries a cane around the school and uses it liberally with the kids.[115]

Another frequent theme was the promise of improved grades or other privileges in return for sex—or threats of failing grades for refusing to perform sexual favors. Girls stated that aggressive sexual advances from their teachers made the school environment oppressive. One seventeen-year-old student from the East Rand stated to a newspaper reporter: "Five teachers have proposed love to me. I told my parents, and I was eventually moved to classes where none of them teach, because I felt very uncomfortable. But there are many other relationships going on between teachers and pupils. It's like you have to pretend to fall in love with them to get A's."[116] One expert told Human Rights Watch:

There are major problems with teachers sexually abusing students, we haven't got quantification for it but there are numerous instances of teachers blackmailing girls—"I'll fail you if you don't have sex with me." Or in the alternative, the girls have sex with teachers to improve their grades. In either event it's an abuse of teacher's powers with significant consequences for other girls in class.[117]

A social worker assisting children in townships outside Durban told Human Rights Watch that she had encountered the problem of teachers demanding sex from girls in exchange for passing marks: "Teachers propose love to girls, and if they don't say yes they say they will fail you."[118] On occasion, students seek out sexual relationships with teachers to gain benefits.

Explaining the challenges of ending teacher sexual abuse, one school official told Human Rights Watch of the difficulties of prohibiting sexual relationships between students and teachers:

Sexual abuse of girls is a problem, but it's far from simple. Age notwithstanding, some students are in consensual relationships with teachers, we might have a seventeen-year-old student and a twenty-

---

[115]Human Rights Watch interview with youth development trainer, Braamfontein, March 17, 2000.
[116]Rowan Philp, "The Worst School in the Country," *Sunday Times*, July 11, 1999.
[117]Human Rights Watch interview with Rachel Jewkes, Acting Director Women's Health Research Unit, Medical Research Council, Pretoria, March 20, 2000.
[118]Human Rights Watch interview with Hlengiwe Magwaza, Childline, Durban, March 28, 2000.

two-year-old teacher, we can't legislate against falling in love. Sometimes the girls initiate a sexual relationship with a teacher in exchange for favors such as good grades or money. They're not so much teachers, as they are clients or johns for some of these girls who are prostituting themselves. I realize it is a big problem—teens are adventurous, engaged in experimenting. Sometimes they go too far and don't know how to get themselves out of situations.[119]

"Dating" Relationships

Human Rights Watch received reports of some teachers having several underage "girlfriends" or attempting to date underage students. A teacher from the Cape Flats outside Cape Town complained to Human Rights Watch that nothing was done after she notified her school administration about a colleague who was having dating relationships at school with underage students. She learned of the abuse when a young female student disclosed the relationship while seeking her advice; the student sought counsel because she learned that the teacher had been "cheating" on her with another one of her classmates.[120]

A social worker assisting schools in townships outside Johannesburg told Human Rights Watch that she encountered an attitude of sexual entitlement among some teachers in her work:

> In 1998, I was at a school near Vilakazi High School. I arrived there, and there were no students. They had left because two teachers had been fighting. One of the teachers wanted to take a standard six girl for himself, and another teacher had said that that was wrong, and they were fighting. I couldn't believe it. I then had to go to another school nearby and I told them what happened. I was saying this was so wrong. That teachers should not be behaving like this. One of the teachers there said to me, "No. The department is not paying us enough money. So this is a fringe benefit. But standard six is too young. Standard nine and ten is where we play."[121]

A township teacher indicated that attitudes were "changing," telling Human Rights Watch, "Teacher on student sexual abuse is a very big problem. In the past it was blatant. Teachers would have sexual relationships with

---

[119] Human Rights Watch interview with Edgar Mushwana, Northern Province member of the executive council (MEC) for Education, Johannesburg, March 24, 2000.
[120] Human Rights Watch interview with teacher, Cape Town, April 14, 2000.
[121] Human Rights Watch interview with youth development trainer, Braamfontein, March 17, 2000.

students openly. They never cared. Things are changing now—at least they try to conceal relationships."[122]

In another incident, a deputy headmaster from a prominent boarding school in KwaZulu-Natal was suspended after being accused of having affairs with three of his students.[123] The girls, the youngest in grade ten, told a meeting of the school's governing body that they had been the deputy headmaster's girlfriends.[124]

Girls who considered themselves to be equal partners in sexual relations with their teachers later found that it was difficult to extricate themselves from the relationship and their teacher's control without changing schools or leaving school altogether.

Rape and Sexual Violence By Students

After the school break, my mom asked me if I wanted to go back to school. I said no. I didn't want to go. All the people who I thought were my friends had turned against me. And they [the rapists] were still there. I felt disappointed. [Teachers] always told me they were glad to have students like me, that they wished they had more students like me. If they had made the boys leave, I wouldn't have felt so bad about it.

WH, age thirteen, gang-raped by classmates

One of the greatest threats to a South African girl's safety at school is likely to be seated next to her in class. South African girls are far more likely to be sexually assaulted by one, or more—usually more—of their male classmates than by a teacher. Sometimes the violence accompanies adolescent dating relationships. At times, girls whom boys perceive to be arrogant or assertive—such as prefects, student leaders, or girls who perform well at school—are targeted for assault or threatened with sexual violence.[125]

---

[122]Human Rights Watch interview with teacher, Johannesburg, March 27, 2000.
[123]Bareng-Batho Kortjaas, "Deputy Principal Suspended for Alleged Affairs with Three Pupils," *Sunday Times*, August 30, 1998.
[124]Ibid.
[125]Male youth participating in research focus groups told researchers that boys rape to "break a woman's pride," or "just to break a girl's dignity" or simply to "teach her a lesson." One youth is quoted as saying: "Girls think that they own the world so the only way to break them is by raping them." "The Culture of Sexual Violence: Youth Views," in Andersson et al, *Beyond Victims and Villains*, p. 59.

V. Sexual Violence in Schools

Girls have been attacked in school toilet facilities, in empty classrooms and hallways, in hostel rooms and dormitories, and in other "no go" areas on school grounds, which girls repeatedly described to us as virtually any place. Sexual assaults were often attempted during class breaks and recess activity times. Human Rights Watch found that boys who commit acts of sexual violence against girls rarely act alone. All of the girls we interviewed who were raped or sexually assaulted by their male classmates said that they had been attacked by two or more boys. We learned of only one case of rape at school committed by a student acting alone.

Girls reported that certain forms of sexual assault occurred in classrooms during class, in full view of their teachers. For instance, girls complained that their male classmates would try to kiss them, fondle their breasts, raise their skirts, and try to touch them under their skirts. Girls reported that such behavior was unwanted, unwelcome, and highly distracting to the learning environment. Girls also complained that aggressive sexual advances made by male students significantly interfered with their ability to study and perform academically at school.

The Case of LB

Nine-year-old LB was raped in the school toilets at her primary school in Guguletu, a township near Cape Town, by two students aged twelve and fourteen in March 2000. She was on her way to the girls' toilet when the two boys intercepted her and took turns raping her in the boys' toilet.[126]

After the rape, LB ran home from school and told her mother. The next day, LB and her mother went to the school and reported the rape to the principal. The principal led LB and her mother from classroom to classroom so that LB could identify her assailants. When confronted with her allegations, the boys admitted to raping LB. Having confirmed that LB had been assaulted, LB's mother took her to the hospital.

The principal convinced LB's family not to press criminal charges against the boys and instead to accept a monetary payment of "seduction damages" from their parents.[127] The principal met with both sets of parents. The parties agreed

---

[126] Human Rights Watch interview, Childline, Guguletu, April 11, 2000.

[127] A rapist or his family often may pay seduction damages to compensate for a rape. A social worker explained:

> Often matters are settled out of court. In situations where parents are educated, criminal complaints are laid. Otherwise, the perpetrator's and victim's family settle the matter financially. This also contributes to cases not being reported. These settlements are not the answer. Often perpetrators say they will pay and never do. In any event, the child never sees any of the money and often doesn't get the

that LB's family would be paid a total of R120 (U.S. $20) in two installments to cover transportation costs for taking the girl to and from the hospital. The principal told LB's parents that they should wait for the parents of the boys to bring the money to the school and the principal would deliver the payment on April 5, 2000. School authorities took no action to counsel or discipline the two boys even after they had admitted assaulting the girl.

When Human Rights Watch interviewed LB's parents on April 11, 2000, they still had not received the full damage payment and were questioning their decision to cooperate with the school principal. LB's father explained that initially:

> We decided not to open a case, we felt we wanted the kids not to be prisoners, not too severely punished. We wanted them to be counseled, taught a lesson. Something must be done to remove the criminal element out of their mind. We were on good terms with their parents. We are not now on good terms. Those kids must feel some pain; they must be educated and taught a lesson. We felt we had to deal with this parent to parent. Now we feel we've moved in the wrong path to be sympathetic, instead it should have been the other way around. They should have been feeling for us. My worry is that the boys are still at a tender age. They're going to grow up, what

---

psychological and emotional support needed after the rape. What may happen is a teenager may rape a girl, he's unemployed so his parents pay the penalty and he never takes responsibility. He doesn't even pay. He learns that he can rape and get away with it. Rape someone and pay R.2,000 and it's over and resolved to the parents, not for the victim. The rapist is going to continue because he knows he did it once and got away with it.

Human Rights Watch interview with Xoliswa Keke, Childline, Durban March 29, 2000.

However, section 9(1)(b) of the 1957 Sexual Offences Act makes it "an offense for any parent or guardian of any child under the age of eighteen years to order, permit, or in any way assist in bringing about, or receiving any consideration for, the defilement, seduction or prostitution of such child." The payment of seduction damages is illegal but observed by custom.

According to Childline, in these cases the person who "brokers" the payment or deal often may take a cut—so for principals, teachers, local chiefs, or policemen to become involved in these payments can also be lucrative for them. Human Rights Watch telephone interview with Joan van Niekerk, Childline, January 12, 2001. For further discussions of customary law see, Thandabantu Nhlapo, "Women's Rights and the Family in Traditional Customary Law," in Susan Bazilli (ed.), *Putting Women on the Agenda* (Johannesburg: Ravan, 1991); H.J. Simons, *African Women: Their Legal Status in South Africa* (London: Hurst, 1968); T.W. Bennett et al (eds.), *African Customary Law* (Cape Town: Juta, 1991).

V. Sexual Violence in Schools

kind of members of society are they going to make. Rape is but one crime. They are small culprits now but they will become big. How can we destroy this in them at a tender age?[128]

LB's mother told Human Rights Watch that she thought the school as well as the parents of the boys should pay damages to her family. She was critical of how the entire incident was handled by the principal, "I don't think the school has organized a meeting about the incident. I think the school committee should be reported to. They need to meet and from the meeting make a decision. They must be made aware of the fact that there is a criminal element at the school."[129] LB's father agreed, "The school's response has not been positive. We are interested in taking further steps. The response from their [the boys'] parents has not been positive."[130]

Because her parents do not have money to send her to another school, LB is still attending the same school as the two boys. The school has taken no steps to counsel or discipline the boys, and has done nothing to further ensure LB's sense of security and well-being in school. A social worker treating LB expressed concern for the child's ability to improve as "she's going back into the same environment" each day. The social worker told Human Rights Watch that LB is "not herself, she's been behaving differently, wetting her bed. She's easily frightened, confused and forgetful."[131] LB's mother told Human Rights Watch: "I can't understand how nobody saw anything or helped my child . . . I don't feel she is safe."[132]

Sexual Assault and Intimidation

They all think that girls are supposed to be their doormat. I think boys must be taught to look at girls as people.

DA, age fifteen

Many attacks appear to be motivated by the desire of male students to control their female classmates or to put down assertive girls. MB told Human

---

[128] Human Rights Watch interview with LB's father, Guguletu, April 11, 2000.
[129] Human Rights Watch interview with LB's mother, Guguletu, April 11, 2000.
[130] Human Rights Watch interview with LB's father, Guguletu, April 11, 2000.
[131] Human Rights Watch interview with Childline, Guguletu, April 11, 2000.
[132] Human Rights Watch interview with LB's mother, Guguletu, April 11, 2000.

Rights Watch about an incident in which two of her male classmates attempted to rape her:

> A group of us had been talking about rape. I said I could take care of myself, I wouldn't be a rape victim. One boy said I couldn't. He said 'give me a chance and I'll prove it.' I told him I wasn't afraid of them and they couldn't hurt me.
>
> One of my friends who is a prefect was working at the media center and I was on my way to see her during break when [they] asked me where I was going and I said to the media center. They asked me if I was going by myself and I told them yes. I started walking there and they followed me. The media center is only about a two minute walk from the main school building but a teacher would not be able to see what goes on there, boys will go there to smoke because they cannot be seen. They started following me and came up behind me and pulled me behind the media center building. I felt like crying. They were trying to take my skirt off and they ripped my top. I had a button missing. There was a stick on the ground. I picked up the stick and started fighting them and they ran away.
>
> He wanted me to know I should be afraid. I am afraid. I think of what if there was no stick on the ground. I think if there was no stick—they would have raped me. I think if the three of us were here in this room as we are now, if they were in this room they could rape me.[133]

Boys use sexual violence to scare girls into submission. One researcher described boy's use of violence as follows: "It's a mode of control over girls, over their bodies, dress, lives, movement social activities, there are a range of ways girls lives are limited by their fear of violence."[134] A girl from Durban explained: "you cannot go to out of bounds areas by yourself."[135]

Nor can girls be assertive or confrontational without risk. AC, a fourteen-year-old student from Mitchell's Plain, told Human Rights Watch that she was beaten by a male classmate for talking back to him.

> A boy beat me up in class while the teacher was out of the room. I was talking with my friend and he came up and asked me what we were talking about. I told him it was none of his business. He pulled

---

[133] Human Rights Watch interview with MB, age seventeen, Durban, April 5, 2000.
[134] Human Rights Watch interview with Sue Goldstone, Soul City, Johannesburg, March 17, 2000.
[135] Human Rights Watch interview with DA, age fifteen, Durban, April 5, 2000.

V. Sexual Violence in Schools

and punched my arm and slapped me on my face. My face and arm were bruised and swollen.[136]

A girl need not be alone or in a "no go" area to be assaulted. The two students who assaulted seventeen-year-old MZ were aged nineteen and twenty at the time of the incident in March 2000, and had been on a drinking binge to celebrate the end of exam period. "It all started at school," MZ told Human Rights Watch.[137] Any female students the two youth encountered during their drinking binge were groped and fondled until they could escape. MZ, already a rape survivor, encountered her two classmates as she was leaving the school grounds after classes with another girlfriend. "He forced me to kiss him and his other friend was putting his hand under my skirt."[138] MZ's friend was also groped and fondled. MZ was eventually able to break away from her two classmates. "When I got home. I was still crying. It makes me so mad. I told [the school officials] because I didn't like it. I just wanted to let them know that it's affected me, it brings back the memories [of being raped]."[139] MZ told Human Rights Watch she had not received medical treatment or counseling after she had been raped.

Some boys demonstrated an intolerance of girls as leaders at school, and used threats of sexual violence in efforts to undermine girls' authority. SW was threatened with sexual violence when she tried to assert her authority as a school prefect. She told Human Rights Watch:

> Last year, when I was on prefect duty, I came across a group of boys gambling with dice on school grounds during a break in violation of school rules. I came up to them and told them to stop gambling. They didn't stop. I told them I was going to take their cards. They told me to go away and stop bothering them. I told them I wasn't going anywhere. Then they threatened me and said they'd have someone rape me and they pulled down their pants. But I stood my ground until the end of break when they stopped gambling and everyone went back to class.[140]

---

[136] Human Rights Watch interview with AC, age fourteen, Mitchell's Plain, April 14, 2000.
[137] Human Rights Watch interview with MZ, age seventeen, Durban, April 4, 2000.
[138] Ibid.
[139] Ibid.
[140] Human Rights Watch interview with SW, age seventeen, Durban, April 5, 2000.

Dating, Relationship, and Retaliation Violence

Hy slaan die liefde in.[141] [He hits the love in.]

They [boys] think it is okay to hit girls. If you see your older brother smoking dagga *[marijuana] and hitting his girlfriend you think it's okay.*

SW, age seventeen

Many girls reported experiencing violence in their intimate relationships or having friends who were experiencing dating violence at school with teachers and said school officials were reluctant to intervene. One student told Human Rights Watch of the problems a friend had with her boyfriend:

[He] beats up his girlfriend; she didn't want to tell on him. He is beating her but she doesn't tell anyone. I only learned of it because I saw her crying at school one day, and she's sort of my friend so I asked her what was wrong and she told me they'd broken up. I think that's why he was beating her. They're back together now, I think, so it's over.[142]

One student described how her boyfriend beat her on two separate occasions at school; she described her abusive relationship in an essay as follows.

One day [my boyfriend] accused me of having a boyfriend behind his back, but I told him that I didn't. I told him if he didn't believe me he must break up with me but he refused. He told me that I must wait for him after school. So I did like he told me, we talked and he started this boyfriend thing and I told him it wasn't true. He didn't believe me. He beat me and left me there crying. The next day at school it was like I was in hell trying not to see [him]. I hated him that day. I couldn't bear to look at him. [Later] he said he was sorry he didn't mean to do it and that he loved me so much he'll never do it again. I believed him. He started accusing me [again] and he was gonna have

---

[141] Human Rights Watch interview with Sue Goldstone, Soul City, Johannesburg, March 17, 2000, quoting an Afrikaans saying.
[142] Human Rights Watch interview with MZ, age seventeen, Durban, April 4, 2000.

V. Sexual Violence in Schools

to teach another lesson. I was scared. The last day at school came and he beat me like he never did before. He told me that he was going to kill me. I apologized and he beat me again and asked me to kiss him and I did because I was scared. I think girls must watch out who they [are] falling in love with and they mustn't trust boys and they must also look after themselves.[143]

Girls also told Human Rights Watch that male students used threats of violence to force girls into unwanted dating and sexual relationships.

When relationship violence occurs at school, little is done by school officials to intervene on behalf of victims. One teacher reported the following incident:

In February a student complained to me that her boyfriend raped her, I had some doubts as to whether or not they were dating. She's fine, coping. The boy is in grade 11 and goes for girls in grade 8 to 10. The school doesn't have evidence. That's why no action has been taken. She reported after two weeks had passed. The boy was suspended from another school. We're trying to help him, he's had problems at home. I've told this girl to go to the CPU [police] but she didn't.[144]

What may begin as battery can escalate to rape. A prosecutor acting in the case of a teenage rape victim explained that the girl's boyfriend was an older student who had been abusive to the girl, even at school, before he raped her:

I've had a case of a fourteen-year-old girl raped at home by an older male student (twenty years old) from her school. He'd hit her openly in front of teachers. They were in a 'relationship.' I learned that the teachers knew of the abuse but were scared to intervene.[145]

Girls at an early age are involved in serious and escalating incidents of partner violence, sometimes this violence occurs at school in plain view of

---

[143]GS, age fifteen, essay on file with the Crime Reduction in Schools Program, University of Natal, Durban.
[144]Interview with teacher, Alexandra township, March 27, 2000.
[145]Human Rights Watch interview with Val Melis, Senior Public Prosecutor, Durban, April 3, 2000.

educators who do not intervene.[146] Apart from having to deal with other dangers at school, cumulatively, such violence creates a hostile environment for girls that is anathema to learning.

Sexual Harassment

It's not flirting, it's uncomfortable.

DA, age fifteen, describing sexual harassment at her school

All the touching at school in class, in the corridors, all day everyday bothers me. Boys touch your bum, your breasts. You won't finish your work because they are pestering you the whole time.

AC, age fourteen, describing sexual harassment at her school

Often some form of sexual harassment[147] will precede a girl's experience of sexual violence.[148] South African girls reported being on the receiving end of

---

[146] For discussions of adolescent relationship violence see, generally, Katharine Wood, Fidelia Maforah and Rachel Jewkes, "'He Forced Me to Love Him': Putting Violence on Adolescent Sexual Health Agendas," in *Social Science and Medicine*, Vol. 47, no. 2 pp. 233-242 (1998); Katharine Wood and Rachel Jewkes, *'Love is a Dangerous Thing': Micro-Dynamics of Violence in Sexual Relationships of Young People in Umtata* (Pretoria: Medical Research Council, 1998); Ravani Chetty, *Gender Conflict Among Adolescents At Rossburgh High School* (Durban: Crime Reduction in Schools Project, 2000).

[147] The Promotion of Equality and Prevention of Unfair Discrimination Act 4 of 2000 defines "harassment" as "unwanted conduct which is persistent or serious and demeans, humiliates or creates a hostile or intimidating environment or is calculated to induce submission…and which is related to sex, gender or sexual orientation."
Promotion of Equality and Prevention of Unfair Discrimination Act, No. 4 of 2000.

[148] See Susan Fineran, Larry Bennett, and Terry Sacco, *Peer Sexual Harassment and Peer Violence Among Adolescents in Johannesburg and Chicago* (Boston University School of Social Work, on file with Human Rights Watch, 2000), a comparative study of peer sexual harassment and violence in South Africa and the United States describing the experience, perpetration, and reaction to such violence for students sixteen to eighteen years of age. The study found that the incidence of physical violence experienced by students in South African schools was "surprisingly high," and that "South African students experienced and perpetrated significantly more physical violence than their [American] counterparts." It concluded that "it may be that violence in South African schools is normative." See also Susan Fineran, *Peer Sexual Harassment and Peer*

V. Sexual Violence in Schools

all manner of unwanted and unwelcome sexual behavior. Adolescent girls told Human Rights Watch that they were most bothered by what they called "flirting" but described as persistent, unwanted fondling or touching by their male classmates.

A sixteen-year-old from Durban told Human Rights Watch: "Most of the boys like flirting, touching you. They'll pretend they only want to talk to you but they're really just trying to touch you. Whenever they're talking they're touching me, that kind of touching makes me feel uncomfortable."[149] Several girls Human Rights Watch interviewed reported that they perceived the touching to be sexual. One girl described to Human Rights Watch how the boys in her school would touch her and other girls: "They'll touch you on your thighs, your butt. They try to touch your breasts."[150] Girls were scared of being blocked or cornered in a sexual way at school. A seventeen-year-old girl told Human Rights Watch: "If I see a group of boys in the corridor, I'll just turn around and find another way to go because I know they'll do something."[151]

Girls complained that students and teachers alike would make sexual comments, jokes, and gestures. An eighteen-year-old student reported: "they stand underneath the stairs to look up your dress and watch you as you go upstairs."[152] Girls complained that boys would show sexual pictures, photographs, and illustrations, or write them sexual messages and graffiti. Girls told Human Rights Watch that boys would call them degrading names, like "slut" and "Isifebe" [Zulu word for slut]. Girls who complained about any unwanted sexual advances were called "lesbians," particularly if they told teachers about the conduct of their classmates.[153]

Female students said that more girls did not complain about this behavior because they are threatened with violence, not because it didn't bother them. One seventeen-year-old student explained: "Sometimes boys threaten you—'if you tell the teacher we will meet you after school and do something to hurt you.'"[154]

Girls described unwanted sexual conduct as persistent and perceived the problem to be "getting worse" with boys becoming bolder. One seventeen-year-old complained: "Even a young boy came up to me trying to kiss me. The grade

---

Violence: South African Children at Risk (Boston University School of Social Work, on file with Human Rights Watch, 2000).
[149] Human Rights Watch interview with DA, age fifteen, Durban, April 5, 2000.
[150] Human Rights Watch interview with SM, age eighteen, Durban, April 5,.2000.
[151] Human Rights Watch interview with NL, age seventeen, Durban, April 5, 2000.
[152] Human Rights Watch interview with SM, age eighteen, Durban, April 5, 2000.
[153] Human Rights Watch interview with Ivan Thompson, teacher, Durban, April 5, 2000.
[154] Human Rights Watch interview with NN, age seventeen, Durban, April 5, 2000.

seven boys copy the grade nine boys."[155] Girls told Human Rights Watch that boys perceived by others to be "popular" were the worst kind of offenders.[156] One girl said that sexual advances made by popular boys sometimes bother her "because they think they're so great that everybody should want them. They just don't believe it when you tell them to leave you alone."[157]

Girls told Human Rights Watch that unwanted and unwelcome sexual behaviors were constant and consistent features of their school experience. AC, a fifteen-year-old girl from the Cape Flats, said that unwanted sexual touching, "happens to most girls, most days" at her school.[158] Another fifteen-year-old girl reported: "this happens every day."[159] According to one study, one in every three schoolgirls in southern Johannesburg said they experienced sexual harassment at school; of those, only 36 percent said they had reported the incident to anyone.[160]

One girl told Human Rights Watch that in her experience, "teachers just ignore it."[161] Girls told Human Rights Watch that they sometimes experienced sexual harassment at school to be overwhelming. One girl explained how the sexual harassment made her feel powerless and frightened: "You tell them [boys] to stop, but the next day, they'll just be doing it again the next day—sometimes it feels scary."[162]

---

[155] Human Rights Watch interview with SM, age eighteen, Durban April 5, 2000
[156] Ann Marie Wolpe, Orla Quinlan, and Lyn Martinez, *Gender Equity in Education: Report of the Gender Equity Task Team* (Pretoria: Department of Education, 1997), p. 95, confirms this view:

> What is increasingly categorized under the label of violence and bullying in schools has been dealt with, in the main, through individualistic psychological approaches which completely neglect the gendered and social dimensions of this behavior. These kinds of approaches promote the belief that individual perpetrators of violent or bullying behaviors do so because of some individually based pathology or low self esteem or social skills, which need to be addressed to stop the behavior. However, ethnographic studies in schools show that many boys identified by the victims as most likely to behave in violent and bullying ways, or as leaders of groups that engaged in these behaviors, are highly competent in social terms and do not lack self confidence. The other factor frequently ignored is the investment boys have in this behavior in terms of the prestige of acceptance it gains in the male club.

[157] Human Rights Watch interview with DA, age fifteen, Durban, April 5, 2000.
[158] Human Rights Watch interview with AC, age fourteen, Mitchell's Plain, April 14, 2000.
[159] Human Rights Watch interview with DA, age fifteen, Durban, April 5, 2000.
[160] Andersson et al, *Beyond Victims and Villains*, p. ix.
[161] Human Rights Watch interview with AC, age fourteen, Mitchell's Plain, April 14, 2000.
[162] Human Rights Watch interview with JI, age sixteen, Durban, April 5, 2000.

Violence in Transit to and from School

Travel to and from school can be a particularly precarious time for girls. Girls who have to travel long distances to school on public transportation are often subjected to threats of sexual violence and sexual harassment in transit. An eighteen-year-old girl described the trials of getting to school safely in a school essay as follows.

> My worst nightmare began in 1998 when I started setting foot in Rossburgh [train] station. Everything was like a fairytale until I experienced the crime myself. Girls being jack rolled [gang-raped] and those who aren't, together with the weaker boys being robbed of their coupons, school jackets, watches and whatever expensive possessions they have is something which I thought occurred in townships ...The station is filled with gangsters. I fear these groups... but I always try not to show them. I have been for a couple of times been [sic] harassed and claimed by certain group members as being their girlfriend. I have also been promised and threatened to be slapped or rather have my ass kicked if I refused any of their dirty demands. Fortunately, the threats remained nothing more than threats.... We could identify them to the teachers and police who merely states that it is for our own good to report them in order to be free from their crimes. The only thing is, they do not know how tough one has to be to risk their lives...we never know when a friend of these thugs is our best friend.[163]

Older adolescent girls told Human Rights Watch that they were not only scared for themselves but that they were particularly afraid for young girls walking to school. A high school student from Alexandra township thought education about rape prevention needed to reach girls in lower grades sooner, explaining "when I was walking to school I saw a man approach a standard three girl to ask her to go with him. I could see she was scared so I stopped, went over and yelled to him: 'What are you doing? She is so young!'"[164] Similarly, Childline has received reports of taxi drivers having isolated young girls by dropping off other passengers first, then abducting the girl and offering her to friends or clients for sex in exchange for money.[165] Poor and black girls are

---

[163] LN, age eighteen, essay on file with the Crime Reduction in Schools Program, University of Natal, Durban.
[164] Human Rights Watch interview, RO, age sixteen, Johannesburg, March 17, 2000.
[165] Human Rights Watch telephone interview with Joan van Niekerk, Childline, Durban, January 12, 2001.

more likely to have to travel long distances by public transport to reach school and are most adversely affected by an increased risk of violence.

VI. CONSEQUENCES OF GENDER VIOLENCE FOR GIRLS' EDUCATION AND HEALTH

Gendered or sex based violence, in the broader context of discrimination, constrains the freedom of movement, choices, and activities of its victims. It frequently results in: intimidation, poor levels of participation in learning activities; forced isolation; low self esteem or self-confidence; dropping out of education or from particular activities or subjects; or other physical, sexual and/or psychological damage. It erodes the basis of equal opportunity realized through equal access to education.[166]

Impact on Girls' Education

My grades are horrible. I'm not doing well because I missed so much school.

PC, age fifteen, describing her school performance after being sexually assaulted by her teacher

The unchallenged occurrence of sexual violence in schools is highly disruptive to girls' education. Left unchecked, sexual violence in schools has a negative impact on the educational and emotional needs of girls and acts as a barrier to attaining education. A school environment where sexual violence is tolerated is one that compromises the right of girls to enjoy education on equal terms with boys. After experiencing violence at school, girls reported losing interest in school, changing schools, or leaving school entirely. The associated health risks posed by sexual violence generally, including unwanted pregnancy and sexually transmitted diseases such as HIV/AIDS, also have implications for girls' educational access.

Education Interrupted
In many instances, girls who have been victims of sexual violence at school leave school for some time, change schools, or even quit attending school entirely, fearing continued abuse from those who have raped, sexually assaulted, or harassed them. Usually teachers and students who are accused of sexual violence remain at school while it is girls who leave. WH, a thirteen-year-old

---

[166] Wolpe, *Gender Equity in Education,* p. 219.

girl from Johannesburg, left her school with plans to go to another because her teacher expected her to sit in the same classroom with the two boys that she alleged had raped her. Similarly, a Johannesburg social worker treating AJ, who was nine when three boys aged thirteen, ten, and nine raped her in the toilets at her school in January 2000, told Human Rights Watch that the girl was no longer attending school because of the assault.[167] AJ's attackers remained at school.

Girls who are victims of sexual violence at school are sometimes motivated to leave school by the hostile treatment they receive from the school community. MC left school when she could no longer endure the ridicule of her classmates after she disclosed that her teacher raped her. Thirteen-year-old WH left school after two of her classmates aged thirteen and fourteen raped her in October 1999. Until then, WH had attended a private school in the northern suburbs of Johannesburg. Excelling as a top student, WH aspired to become a lawyer. For the time being she has deferred this dream, too intimidated by the presence of her attackers to return to school. WH told Human Rights Watch: "I left [school] because I was raped by two guys in my class who were supposedly my friends."[168] When Human Rights Watch interviewed WH in March 2000, she was being home schooled by her mother and contemplating switching to an all girls school after the conclusion of the rape trial.

WH told Human Rights Watch the boys would seek her out and taunt her during breaks in class, and that when no teachers were around, the boys would talk loudly to the other students so she could hear them, denying the rape ever took place. WH's classmates also started to tease her and call her a liar. Unable to cope, and feeling that all her friends had turned against her, WH left school a week after the rape: "I haven't had any contact with school or my friends or teacher since November. It's hard losing your friends."[169]

In another account, a seventeen-year-old girl from Mitchell's Plain was raped by four of her classmates in an empty classroom just after school while a fifth boy watched. The school took no action until the story appeared in the media. The four boys who raped the girl were reportedly suspended for "having sex on school property" after claiming the girl consented. The fifth boy was not disciplined.[170] Unable to cope with constant harassment from her other

---

[167]Human Rights Watch interview with Shamona Reddy, social worker, Johannesburg Reception Assessment and Referral Center, March 23, 2000.
[168]Human Rights Watch interview with WH, age thirteen, Johannesburg, March 15, 2000.
[169]Ibid.
[170]Andy Duffy, "No Tears for Gang Raped Schoolgirl," *Mail and Guardian*, November 19, 1997.

VI. Consequences of Gender Violence for Girls' Education and Health

classmates and the indifference of the school administration after she reported the rape, the girl left the school.[171]

Some girls change schools rather than remaining in a non-supportive and even hostile environment. A Durban social worker told Human Rights Watch about one of her clients who changed schools after four boys from her school raped her.

> One of my cases attended school in Chatsworth. She was fourteen at the time she was raped in 1998. She was gang-raped by four to five older boys from her school, on the quad. She was forced to do oral sex. The rape was reported to the principal who called her parents. Her parents and her brother did not believe her. If it happened, it was her fault. The boys were friends of her brother. They are all still at school. The girl has been transferred to a different school. She is suicidal and not eating.[172]

Girls who must temporarily leave school or change schools to avoid abusive classmates or teachers experience disruptions in their education. Girls reported that missing school had a negative impact on their school performance. One student explained: "I didn't go back to school for one month [after being sexually abused by her teacher], I just wanted to be alone."[173] Many victims of sexual violence at school miss some school trying to cope with what has happened to them and find they cannot catch up with their course work.

Diminished School Performance

Girls who are victims of rape and other forms of sexual violence often struggle with physical and emotional trauma that leaves them unable to do their school work or view school as a priority.[174] Girls indicated to Human Rights Watch that the sexual violence they experienced at school had a negative impact on their school performance and their desire to go to school. Human Rights Watch repeatedly encountered girls who said that they could no longer focus on their work or view school as important. One fifteen-year-old student described

---

[171] Ibid.

[172] Human Rights Watch interview with Andrea Engelbrecht, Childline, Durban, March 28, 2000.

[173] Human Rights Watch interview with PC, age fifteen, Johannesburg, March 18, 2000.

[174] For a discussion on the educational, emotional, and behavioral impact of sexual harassment in primary and secondary schools, consult Nan Stein, *Classrooms and Courtrooms: Facing Sexual Harassment in K-12 Schools* (New York: Teachers College Press, Columbia University, 1999).

her school performance after she was raped by her teacher as follows: "I did badly in school. First term [before the rape] I passed with flying colors, but second term I did badly. I got conditional transfer. Third and fourth term were also bad."[175]

This girl told Human Rights Watch that since she was raped: "I feel less interested. I want to leave school. We were told that we could leave school after standard seven, so that's what I want to do. I want to leave and go…I just don't like it [school], the kids, the teachers."[176] Girls said they did not want to go to school, they did not want to participate in class, and they found it hard to pay attention in class. Students also said they felt betrayed by their schools.

Girls told Human Rights Watch that it was hard to attend school and face others or to focus on course work after experiencing sexual violence at school. After two male classmates sexually assaulted and attempted to rape seventeen-year-old MB at school, she told Human Rights Watch:

> I felt like leaving this school, I cried. I feel horrible because before all this happened they were my friends. I was thinking how am I going to face these guys. We attend classes together. How am I going to be myself like before? How am I going to be the same again? I asked advice from my mother she said I must try to calm myself down. I had to write my exams. So I just calmed myself down and tried to forgive them. I passed my exams, but it was hard. I still feel bad but I just take it out of my mind. I would leave this school if I could.[177]

The trauma of sexual abuse can affect a child's ability to concentrate.[178] A social worker treating one child told Human Rights Watch how the child's school performance suffered after the rape, "She was a brilliant student, also an athlete. She failed matric. She dropped all athletic activities."[179]

Emotional and Behavioral Impact

As a result of sexual abuse, girls often have negative and confused thoughts and beliefs about themselves. MC, who was fifteen when she was

---

[175] Human Rights Watch interview with MC, age fifteen, Johannesburg, March 18, 2000. MC explained that "conditional transfer" means she failed, but that the school decided to pass her anyway.

[176] Human Rights Watch interview with MC, age fifteen, Johannesburg, March 18, 2000.

[177] Human Rights Watch interview with MB, age seventeen, April 5, 2000.

[178] See "The Impact: Educational, Emotional, Behavioral," in Stein, *Classrooms and Courtrooms*, and sources cited therein.

[179] Human Rights Watch interview with Mallory Issacs, Childline, Cape Town, April 14, 2000.

VI. Consequences of Gender Violence for Girls' Education and Health 65

raped by her teacher early in 1999, told Human Rights Watch: "After he raped me, I felt ugly. I didn't know what to do, like it was all my fault...I couldn't sleep."[180] FH observed that her daughter changed after she was raped.

> [My daughter] cannot handle what's happened, as much as she tries not to show it. I know her, and I see that it's really eating her. She says to me, "but mom, how can you understand?" I tell her that I do understand. That what happened to her happened to me because I'm her mother. She's a part of me. It's hurting me because she's a part of me.[181]

A counselor described the emotional state of a sixteen-year-old student who phoned Childline in March 2000 to report that her teacher had raped her. The girl had said that she believed she was raped for being a bad student. The counselor noted that the girl "sounded expressionless when she related her rape. Since then she cannot concentrate, sleep properly, etc. She reflects feelings of guilt about...everything being her fault." [182]

Children's behavior pattern often changes drastically when they are subjected to abuse. Sexually abused children may become aggressive, develop eating disorders, suffer insomnia, run away, and attempt or commit suicide.[183] In June 1998, an anonymous father called Childline to report suspected sex abuse by a teacher against his eleven-year-old daughter.

> Father was distressed about his eleven-year-old daughter who sent a fax to her nineteen-year-old teacher stating "hello bitch you must get another fucking hole bitch." The school principal brought the fax to the attention of the father who spoke to his daughter. She admitted to writing the letter in anger because the teacher was touching her in places she is not supposed to be touched. The daughter is not communicating much, withdrawn and schoolwork has gone from good to not too good.[184]

---

[180] Human Rights Watch interview with MC, age fifteen, March 18, 2000.
[181] Human Rights Watch interview with WH's mother, March 15, 2000.
[182] Childline call record, March, 2000.
[183] See "The Impact: Educational, Emotional, Behavioral" in Stein, *Classrooms and Courtrooms*, and sources cited therein.
[184] Childline call report, June 1998.

After an abusive encounter, children experience anger, depression, and feelings of isolation, ambivalence, anxiety, guilt, and hopelessness.[185] PC's depression colored her view of the world and education generally, she told Human Rights Watch: "I don't want to be there [at school]. I just don't care anymore. I don't have motivation anymore. I thought about changing schools, but why? If it can happen here it can happen any place and the response will be the same. I didn't want to go back to any school."[186]

Impact on Girls' Health

Unwanted Pregnancy and Pregnancy Discrimination

Some teachers don't treat pregnant girls okay. . . . I want to stay in school, I want to give me and my baby a bright future.

YP, pregnant seventeen-year-old

Unwanted pregnancy is a possible complication that may result from rape in any context. RH, a standard nine student from Impendle in KwaZulu-Natal, called Childline in 1999, for assistance. She had become pregnant after her teacher coerced her into a sexual relationship and has had to leave school as a consequence.

> [RH] called very distressed. She mentioned that she was sexually abused by a teacher at school. He threatened her that if she refused him he would fail her or have her expelled from school. The abuse continued until she fell pregnant last year. She had a baby at the beginning of the year—but it died immediately after birth. While she was pregnant the teacher came to pay the guardians for damages and to keep them quiet about this incident. The principal of the school is aware of this but has not done anything to help the child. [RH] would like to go back to school but the same teacher has been threatening to kill her if she comes back to school. He is presently threatening her for telling people that he was the father of the baby. She would like someone to help her. Her parents/guardians are aware of this but are unable to protect her.[187]

---

[185]See, generally, Tinka Labuschagne, *A Guide to the Effective Management of Child Sexual Abuse*, (Johannesburg: Johannesburg Community Chest, 1998).
[186]Human Rights Watch interview with PC, age fifteen, March 18, 2000.
[187]Childline case record, April 1999.

VI. Consequences of Gender Violence for Girls' Education and Health 67

RH's unwanted pregnancy meant the end of her education.

Human Rights Watch is concerned that among other forms of sex discrimination that may hinder girls' education in South Africa, the exclusion of pregnant girls from education equal to that of others is problematic. South Africa law and the Convention on the Elimination of All Forms of Discrimination Against Women prohibit the exclusion from school of pregnant girls.[188] Nevertheless, some schools continue to exclude pregnant girls in violation of the law.[189]

Human Rights Watch interviewed a number of pregnant girls about how pregnancy had impacted their access to education.[190] Human Rights Watch talked with two girls who said they were told to leave their prior schools after their pregnancies were discovered. One student told Human Rights Watch, "my teacher told me I must stay at home, I can't come to school being pregnant."[191] DM reported her school's response to her pregnancy as follows:

> The school found out I was pregnant when my father told the principal. I'd told my teacher and she said 'you are not supposed to be here pregnant.' The principal told my father, 'we don't need girls like yours, we don't need girls who are pregnant.'[192]

---

[188] Prohibitions against pregnancy discrimination are contained in Section 8 of the Promotion of Equality and Prevention of Unfair Discrimination Act 4 of 2000. The South African constitution provides: "The state may not unfairly discriminate directly or indirectly against anyone on one or more grounds, including…pregnancy." Section 9 (3) of the Constitution of South Africa Act 108 of 1996.

[189] Human Rights Watch interview with Ruta van Niekerk, Principal Hospitaalskool, Pretoria, March 20, 2000. See also, Nokuthula Masuku, "Pregnant Schoolgirls Must Go," in *Agenda*, no. 37, 1998, p. 37-38; FAWE, *Girls Education: The Trap of Adolescent Pregnancy* (Nairobi: Forum for African Women Educationalists, undated); Connie Selebogo, "The Rights of the Pregnant Learner," *The Teacher (Mail and Guardian)*, July 26, 2000. In 1999, 17,000 babies were born to South African mothers aged sixteen and younger.

[190] When we interviewed the girls they were attending a special school for pregnant girls in Pretoria affiliated with a hospital. It should be noted that one condition of the interviews with students was that we not inquire as to how they became pregnant or the fathers of their children. Therefore, Human Rights Watch does not represent that any of the student pregnancies were unwanted nor do we suggest that the pregnancies are the result of school-based rape.

[191] Human Rights Watch interview with NS, age seventeen, Pretoria, March 20, 2000.

[192] Human Rights Watch interview with DM, age sixteen, Pretoria, March 20, 2000.

DM remained under the impression that "it is a rule of the school that pregnant girls cannot attend." While DM had been unaware of her rights, "I was having no choice in the matter, if they would have let me I'd have stayed." She did perceive her treatment as unfair. She complained, "boys who make girls pregnant aren't asked to leave school."[193]

NS, who was asked to leave school because of her pregnancy, also thought she had no right to remain in school—that it was public policy for pregnant students to leave school:

> One of my friends told me 'it is the rule of the school' that pregnant girls must stay home. I know this to be true because other girls I know from my school who fell pregnant stayed home. I think the education department should change the rules.[194]

Some girls were uncertain as to whether they would continue their studies or be allowed to return to their former schools: "I don't know if I'll continue my studies, I'm thinking about whether to continue and do matric."[195] Most girls expressed an intention and desire to return to school; a few expressed apprehensions about returning to their old schools for fear of ridicule, while others were not sure they would be wanted. One girl explained: "I've heard of so many girls who haven't been allowed back. I'm scared. I think I have a 50-50 chance of being accepted back."[196]

It is striking that students who have raped their female classmates go to school without interruption, but should a girl get pregnant she must worry about her educational prospects.

Risk of Sexually Transmitted Infections

Compounding the high rate of sexual violence against girls in South Africa is the country's rapidly accelerating rate of HIV/AIDS infection. Rape and other forms of sexual violence place girls at risk of contracting sexually transmitted infections, including the HIV/AIDS virus. HIV/AIDS-associated illnesses are taking a toll on the education system and disrupt education for all students, but especially girls.

UNAIDS, the joint United Nations program on HIV/AIDS,[197] estimates that about half of all fifteen-year-olds in the African countries worst affected by

---

[193] Human Rights Watch interview with DM, age sixteen, Pretoria, March 20, 2000.
[194] Human Rights Watch interview with NS, age seventeen, Pretoria, March 20, 2000.
[195] Human Rights Watch interview with ML, age seventeen, Pretoria, March 20, 2000.
[196] Human Rights Watch interview with RG, age seventeen, Pretoria, March 20, 2000.
[197] UNAIDS brings together seven U.N. agencies to advocate for global action on HIV/AIDS. Represented agencies include the United Nations Children's Fund, the

VI. Consequences of Gender Violence for Girls' Education and Health 69

AIDS will eventually die of the disease. South Africa is one of those worst affected countries, with an infection rate of 19.9 percent, and AIDS is expected to kill half those who are now fifteen years old.[198] The HIV infection rate in South Africa has increased to19.9 percent from 12.9 percent two years ago.[199]

Each year, many children and women in South Africa are infected with HIV when they are raped.[200] The risk of virus transmission during rape is high. Girls have a higher risk than boys of contracting the virus from sexual intercourse, willing or unwilling.[201] The ease of transmission may be greater for girls for several reasons. Biologically, HIV is transmitted more readily from man to woman than from woman to man. Girls are much more likely to be

---

United Nations Development Program, the United Nations Population Fund, the United Nations International Drug Control Programme, the United Nations Educational, Scientific and Cultural Organization, the World Health Organization, and the World Bank.

[198] Lawrence K. Altman, "U.N. Warning AIDS Imperils Africa's Youth," *New York Times*, June 28, 2000.

[199] Joint United Nations Programme on HIV/AIDS, *Report on the Global HIV/AIDS Epidemic* (Geneva, UNAIDS, June 2000). See also Altman, "AIDS Imperils Africa's Youth," *New York Times*; UNAIDS/WHO Working Group on Global HIV/AIDS and STI Surveillance, *South Africa: Epidemiological Fact Sheet on HIV/AIDS and Sexually Transmitted Infections* (Geneva, World Health Organization, 2000); HIV Insite, *South Africa: Context of the Epidemic*, available at http://hivinsite.ucsf.edu/international/africa/ (accessed at February 13,2001).

[200] Rachel Jewkes, *The HIV/AIDS Emergency: Department of Education Guidelines for Educators* (Pretoria: Department of Education, 2000), p. 6. Insurance companies in South Africa have launched "rape survivor" polices. For twenty-five rands per month women, children, and men can insure themselves for up to R.5,000 for rape. Typically policies cover medical and psychiatric treatment for the survivor, including the provision of anti-retroviral drug regimens to prevent HIV transmission. Lisa Vetten, "Paper Promises, Protest and Petitions: South African State and Civil Society Responses to Violence Against Women," in Yoon Jung Park, Joanne Fedler, and Zubeda Dangor (eds.), *Reclaiming Women's Spaces* (Johannesburg: Nisaa Institute for Women's Development, 2000), p. 108.

[201] The AIDS Law Project and Tshwaranang Legal Advocacy Centre report that violence against women, including domestic violence and rape, is strongly linked to a woman's exposure to sexually transmitted infections such as HIV/AIDS. Women who have little control in sexual interactions are those most at risk of contracting the virus from non-consensual or unprotected sexual intercourse. Corresponding with biological vulnerability is the fact that women have fewer contraceptive choices, unequal health care access, and women are far more likely to be coerced into sex or raped. Girls are more vulnerable. Betsi Pendry, "The Links Between Gender Violence and HIV/AIDS," in *Agenda*, no. 39, 1998, pp. 30-33.

infected during unprotected vaginal intercourse with an infected partner than are boys. When sex is coerced, there is less likely to be secretion of vaginal fluids associated with sexual arousal; for very young girls, pre-pubescent children, there is no secretion of vaginal fluids. In the case of gang rape, where violence and other trauma and injury, such as vaginal tearing, is probable, the likelihood of becoming infected with a sexually transmitted disease may be significantly higher.

According to UNAIDS, the infection rates in young African women are far higher than those in young men, with HIV infection rates more than five times as high among African teenage girls as among teenage boys.[202] South African health officials say adolescent girls are twice as likely to become infected with HIV as boys, a reflection of their increased sexual activity, often coerced, with older men who have had longer exposure to the virus. In South Africa, the prevalence rate of HIV in girls and young women aged fifteen to twenty-four is almost twice that of boys and young men of the same age.[203]

The cost of HIV/AIDS to education for all children is high. Girls' education will likely be disproportionately and negatively affected by the AIDS epidemic whether or not they are infected; girls are also most likely to care for a sick family member and manage the household.[204]

---

[202] UNAIDS, *Global HIV/AIDS Epidemic* p. 11.
[203] Ibid., p. 125.
[204] The epidemic is also decreasing family income, reducing the money available for school fees, and increasing the pressure on children to drop out of school. It is also adding to the number of children who are growing up without the support of parents, which also may affect a child's ability to stay in school. See Joint United Nations Programme on HIV/AIDS, *Report on the Global HIV/AIDS Epidemic* (Geneva, UNAIDS, June 2000).

VII. THE SCHOOL RESPONSE

I don't think they [the school administration] really know how it affects us. Maybe to them it is just a big joke—but to me—it is not to me. I was not laughing or playing. It's not a joke or game—it really bothers me.

MZ, age seventeen, sexually assaulted at school

Girls described a persistent response pattern whereby schools discounted their reports of sexual violence and harassment or failed to respond with any degree of seriousness. Girls were discouraged from reporting abuse to school officials for a variety of reasons, not the least of which was the hostile and indifferent responses they received from their school communities. Sometimes school officials appear to have failed to respond adequately because they simply did not know what to do; other times they ignored the problem; still other times they appear to have been afraid to assist. In many instances, schools actively discouraged victims of school-based gender violence from alerting anyone outside the school or accessing the justice system. In the worst cases, school officials concealed the existence of violence at their schools and failed to cooperate fully with authorities outside the school system.

The sad consequence of such responses is that the problem is often placed squarely on the shoulders of girls. Many girls have come to accept that sexual violence and harassment simply must be endured if they are attending school. The failure of school authorities to respond allows perpetrators of gender violence to act with impunity and reinforces sex discrimination in schools. By contrast, when schools responded to girls who reported abuse by supporting them, investigating their claims, and confronting their attackers, girls reported feeling safe and empowered.

Barriers to Reporting Abuse

The difficulty girls face in reporting abuse is the first barrier school officials must overcome in order to adequately respond to the problem of sexual violence. Many opportunities to intervene and prevent escalation of certain behaviors into violence are missed because girls for a variety of reasons fail to report sexual violence. Girls told Human Rights Watch that after they reported abuse not only were they not supported, they were ridiculed and became the object of vicious rumors at their schools. Many girls said they were afraid to pursue their complaints for fear of further violence; other girls simply felt reporting would be futile.

Fear is a major factor affecting whether or not a girl will report abuse. Many children are afraid to come forward or disclose when teachers abuse them because teachers use violence and threats of violence to intimidate children into silence. MN, fifteen years old, phoned Childline in September 1999 to report that her teacher had been sexually abusing her. The intake operator summarized the call as follows.

> Caller's teacher abuses her. Always orders her to remain behind for maths...then follows to abuse her. Caller couldn't tell someone, teacher said nobody will believe her. Only her friend knows about this. Caller feels sad, scared and confused.[205]

A mother called Childline in August 1997 to report that her daughter had been sexually abused at school by a trainee teacher and that she struggled to help her child overcome her fears of disclosing the abuse. The call record notes:

> Mother called re her child [who] was being sexually abused by a student teacher. [M]other did complain to the principal and she was requested to write a letter which will be sent to the department. [The teacher] scolded her [the child] and threatened to hit her. [N]ow the child is afraid to give any further details. Mom wanted to know if it will be okay for the child to call one of the counselors.[206]

Experts and social workers we interviewed told us that teachers use their status and authority to intimidate children into sexual relations.[207] Fear keeps many children quiet about abuse, one social worker explained:

> Sex abuse by teachers is there, it just goes unreported. People look up to teachers. Even if a child knows it's wrong, they are confused. If I tell—the teacher may fail me or hit me. Corporal punishment remains a problem in schools. Kids fear that they won't be believed and fear what may happen to them if they tell.[208]

---

[205] Childline call record, September 1999.
[206] Childline call record, August 1997.
[207] Human Rights Watch interview with Tinka Labuschagne, Say No to Child Abuse Alliance, Johannesburg, March 16, 2000.
[208] Human Rights Watch interview with Xoliswa Keke, Childline, Durban, March 29, 2000.

VII. The School Response

Similarly, most girls do not complain about the bulk of abuse inflicted on them by male classmates because, as one girl explained, "girls are too shy or too scared to speak up."[209] Girls are not only afraid of continued violence, but also the negative reactions of their peers. When two classmates sexually assaulted seventeen-year-old MZ, a girl attending a Durban metropolitan area high school, she bravely alerted school authorities, putting aside peer pressure not to speak out, but later questioned her decision and even felt she had to justify her decision to speak out to her friends. MZ explained: "My friend didn't even want to report it. She said it was no big deal. Others thought so too. It's not affected us in the same way, she's over it. She says they were drunk and we should just forget about it—but I can't forget."[210] Although the two students sexually assaulted several girls at school that day, MZ was the only one who came forward. "I can't say my friends have been supportive, but I am coping."[211]

Some girls who did report abuse to school officials said they feared violent retaliation from their attackers and, feeling powerless, chose not to press their claims. A seventeen-year-old girl who elected not to pursue formal charges against her classmates after an attempted rape because she feared them explained: "The teacher asked me if she could tell the police. I told her that they'll be expelled and they'll wait at the bus and do something bad to me because of me they'll have been expelled. So I'll just forgive them. So we just made the case dissolve."[212] She accepted having little control over the situation because she could not confront the boys on their terms, explaining her decision to Human Rights Watch: "They apologized and I told them I forgive them. I must forgive them. There is no choice. I didn't want to forgive them. Because I'm a girl I can't fight them." Having learned submission as a survival skill and accepting that no one could keep her safe, MB simply took it as her place as a girl to be the object of violence.

Counselors assisting child victims of sexual abuse maintain that the way girls are treated after a rape or sexual assault by their peers, teachers, school officials, and sometimes even their friends and family, is the reason why most attacks go unreported.[213] Girls feel they are not valued when they perceive attacks against them are not taken seriously by school administrators. The lack of proportionality in the punishment of attacks emboldens students who would perpetrate violence against others.

---

[209] Human Rights Watch interview with DA, age fifteen, Durban, April 5, 2000.
[210] Human Rights Watch interview with MZ, age seventeen, Durban, April 4, 2000.
[211] Ibid.
[212] Human Rights Watch interview with MB, age seventeen, Durban, April 5, 2000.
[213] Human Rights Watch interview with Lynn Cawood, Childline, Johannesburg, March 14, 2000.

The silence surrounding sexual violence for many girls grows into a resigned acceptance that unwanted and unwelcome sexual behaviors simply must be endured in educational settings. Girls learn to acquiesce to the violence because often they receive little support from their peers at school or from school officials.

Indifferent or Inadequate Response

The abuse girls experience at school is often magnified by the reactions they receive when they report abuse to school officials. Girls who did report abuse told Human Rights Watch that school officials responded with indifference, disbelief, and hostility. Schools that do not take sexual violence and harassment seriously provide support for those who would commit violence against girls.

Many girls feel it is of little use to report problems, having learned that in most instances little or nothing will be done to their male classmates by school authorities, so the abuse continues. One girl explained: "They [boys who abuse] are happy to stay home. They enjoy being suspended, it's their favorite thing. By doing something stupid at school they have a free day off and in the end they just come back and do the same thing again anyway."[214] Another girl expressed her frustration about the futility of speaking out; "I don't report anything anymore. I feel it's unnecessary. I'm just wasting my time."[215]

Dissatisfied with her school's response to her sexual assault complaint, MZ told Human Rights Watch that she questioned her decision to come forward. Contemplating whether she had done the right thing by bringing the incident to the attention to school administrators, MZ said: "I don't know, maybe, I'm still trying to figure out what to do. I wanted to show them that they can't get away with everything. I think more should have been done to them after what they did. If there was something I could do, I'd have done it long ago."[216]

AC, a fourteen-year-old pupil at a school in Mitchell's Plain, near Cape Town, no longer questions whether she should report violence to school officials. As she told Human Rights Watch, she knows better than to bother. AC felt her concerns were simply disregarded by school administrators when she complained to a school official about being beaten up by a boy in class after "talking back to him."

> I left class and went to the principal's office and told. The principal told me to "go back to class and bring the boy here to the office." I

---

[214] Human Rights Watch interview with NN, age seventeen, Durban, April 5, 2000.
[215] Human Rights Watch interview with AC, age fourteen, Mitchell's Plain, April 15, 2000.
[216] Human Rights Watch interview with MZ, age seventeen, Durban, April 4, 2000.

VII. The School Response

went back to class and told him the principal wanted to see him, but he didn't come. So I went back to the principal's office. He told me to go back and tell him he'd be expelled if he didn't come to the office. So finally he came, and all the principal told him was "stop—if you're beating girls already you'll grow up to beat your wife." He didn't get detention. Nothing. I don't report anything anymore. I feel it's unnecessary. I'm just wasting my time.[217]

AC is not so much afraid of violence as she is resigned that it is simply a reality of her education experience.

Girls reported that unwanted, controlling, abusive, and humiliating interactions including sexual assault and harassment are still viewed as a game by some boys, and not taken seriously by school authorities.[218] One fifteen-year-old student told Human Rights Watch that boys treated sexual harassment as a game: "When you tell them to 'stop', when you say 'no,' they are just laughing and keep on doing the same thing."[219]

When boys are confronted by school officials with allegations of sexual assault, girls repeatedly said that boys will claim they were just 'joking' or 'playing,' and then expect the explanation to suffice. Too often it does. One seventeen-year-old girl told Human Rights Watch about the reaction of her classmates when confronted by her allegations of attempted rape: "I told a teacher about what happened...They told the teacher they were just playing. But they weren't just playing because they were serious. They weren't playing when they were hitting me and ripping my clothes."[220] Her attackers were not disciplined.

Human Rights Watch did meet with one school official who asserted that he responded promptly and decisively to the problems of sexual violence and harassment in his school. He told us that the school had gone so far as to recently suspend two boys who sexually assaulted female students. The school granted our request to interview one of the students assaulted, seventeen-year-old MZ. She confirmed that the school had in fact suspended the two boys who attacked her—but for only three days. MZ did not feel that she was taken seriously after she reported the incident, nor did she feel the school's response was sufficient. The action was not enough to make MZ feel better, as she still

---

[217] Human Rights Watch interview with AC, age fourteen, Mitchell's Plain, April 15, 2000.
[218] Andersson, *Beyond Victims and Villains*, p 56. One in every ten male youths surveyed in CIETafrica's study thought jack-rolling or "magintsa" [gang rape] was "cool."
[219] Human Rights Watch interview with NJ, age sixteen, Durban, April 5, 2000.
[220] Human Rights Watch interview with MB, age seventeen, Durban, April 5, 2000.

must confront her attackers every day at school: "They are back here right now—when I see them I feel like vomiting. They aren't in matric so they'll be around for some time."[221]

In other cases, schools may not respond at all. An anonymous boy called Childline in July 1997 on behalf of his sister to report that a teacher was sexually abusing her at her school in Chatsworth.[222] Instead of expressing concern when confronted with allegations by a Childline counselor, the school gave no credence to the charge. The investigating counselor noted: "I called the school. Spoke to the principal, he laughed at the allegations—because the alleged perpetrator is the vice-principal of the school."[223]

Ostracizing and Marginalizing Victims

When [MC] went through hell at school that made it easier for me to come forward [to police] because I knew I wasn't the only one. I thought if you're the only one it is your word against his.

PC, age fifteen

The injury does not end with the assault for girls who report or speak out against violence. Girls fear ridicule and rejection by the school community. When girls come forward, they are often ridiculed and rejected by their peers, male and female alike. For instance, the boys who were alleged to have raped thirteen-year-old WH would tease her at school. Other students would call her "liar." After WH brought charges against her rapists, she told Human Rights Watch that "All the people who I thought were my friends had turned against me."[224] WH's mother told Human Rights Watch that other students would call their home and harass her daughter. WH's teacher allegedly spread rumors about WH and the merits of the case against the boys.[225] WH felt cast out by the school administration while no action was taken by the school against the alleged perpetrators.

A recently retired teacher explained that in her experience schools do not aid victims of violence: "Schools find sexual abuse embarrassing and oftentimes will attempt to sweep it under the carpet. The survivor is left to swim or sink,

---

[221] Human Rights Watch interview with MZ, age seventeen, Durban, April 4, 2000.
[222] Childline call record, July 1997.
[223] Ibid.
[224] Human Rights Watch interview with WH, age thirteen, Johannesburg, March 18, 2000.
[225] Human Rights Watch interview with WH's mother, March 18, 2000.

VII. The School Response

there are no support structures designed to assist. The victim runs a risk of not being believed, ostracized, or being ridiculed."[226] Often the hostility is severe enough for children to simply drop their allegations, one social worker explained:

> I had a case of a series of girls who were being fondled at school by a teacher. Two girls spoke up, but then one withdrew her complaint. The other child received no support from the other teachers or the school community. It's too much for a child to pursue alone. In the end the teacher responded: "she's just accusing me because she has a crush on me."[227]

Girls also reported that their classmates and sometimes school officials ridiculed and rejected them after they came forward and schools did nothing to intervene.

Lack of Procedures and Ignorance of Existing Policy

Human Rights Watch interviewed South African teachers, school principals, education policy experts, and social workers concerning policies to address sexual violence in schools. They uniformly said they were unaware of any standard procedural guidelines provided to schools by the national or provincial education departments on how schools should treat those who are accused of sexual violence or harassment or accommodate victims of sexual violence in their schools. Human Rights Watch contacted the national Department of Education and the provincial departments of areas where we documented abuses to inquire about gender violence policies. We were unable to obtain a copy of any policy guidelines specifically addressing the problem of sexual violence in schools from the national department. Only the Western Cape education department responded that it was nearing completion of a gender violence policy.

School employees Human Rights Watch interviewed complained that they had not received procedures or guidance about how to address gender violence in their schools and called for increased assistance on the issue. One consultant working with the Western Cape education department and counseling adolescent

---

[226] Human Rights Watch interview with Sthokozo Nxumalo, Resources Aimed At the Prevention of Child Abuse and Neglect (RAPCAN), Cape Town, April 17, 2000. RAPCAN is a nongovernmental organization committed to developing child abuse prevention strategies to combat patterns of abuse through training and advocacy.
[227] Human Rights Watch interview with Linda Dhabicharam, Childline, Durban, March 28, 2000.

rape victims in the area observed: "Teachers haven't been prepared for it, schools don't know how to handle it, and above all schools don't want their name tarnished."[228] Emphasizing the need for expanded training on sexual violence issues, a teacher from Mitchell's Plain agreed: "We're not equipped, but I just go on my instincts. There's no guidance."[229] While the instincts of some teachers are better than others, a girl's safety at school should not depend on a teacher's instincts, but rather on clear procedures to address complaints of sexual violence.

A vice principal of a school in Cato Manor, near Durban, also told Human Rights Watch that her school lacked procedures, "No, we weren't given a procedure on how to deal with abuse from the Department of Education."[230] A former teacher who had worked in five different schools over a period of fourteen years in KwaZulu-Natal summed up the situation in her experience as follows:

> In black schools in the townships, there is definitely no formal effort to evaluate the problem. At times it is not even viewed as a problem worthy of attention at all. In some areas it is seen as a great privilege for a child to be at school at all. There are far more urgent issues to worry about such as shelter and food than to be worried about children's rights. So there are no standard procedures for reporting abuse. Pupils, should they be brave enough, will approach any teacher on the issue, like they would on any other issue, and it may be ignored.[231]

Students are also without guidance. Schools have made few efforts to inform children and parents of their rights and the responsibilities of their school in developmentally appropriate language.

The lack of a broadly disseminated policy on sexual violence has resulted in considerable confusion among school management on how to confront the problem. Some teachers expressed a desire to help their students, but felt they could not or did not know how to do so. Misconceptions abounded about what a school could or should do to prevent, investigate and punish sexual violence. For example, one educator was under the impression that "if a parent doesn't

---

[228] Human Rights Watch interview with Ursula Higgins, youth advocate, Cape Town, April 12, 2000.
[229] Human Rights Watch interview with Sharon Moore, teacher, April 14, Cape Town 2000.
[230] Human Rights Watch interview with vice principal, Cato Manor, April 5, 2000.
[231] Human Rights Watch interview with Sthokozo Nxumalo, RAPCAN, Cape Town, April 7, 2000.

VII. The School Response

want to go to police [about a rape] there is nothing we can do because these things occur. I don't think we can do anything [to the accused] until he's proven guilty, we cannot just expel or suspend him because the parents can sue us."[232] Because of the failure of the national and provincial education departments to promptly establish and to broadly disseminate a comprehensive policy or procedural guidelines, gaps remain in efforts to prevent, investigate, and punish sexual violence in schools.

Some key problems we identified associated with the lack of a widely disseminated and actively enforced policy to end sexual violence and harassment of girls at school include: victims remain in classes with offenders and are ostracized and ridiculed by other students; victims leave school due to the hostile environment and indifference to their needs after assault; offending teachers and students are not disciplined or prosecuted; teachers who have repeatedly engaged in sexual misconduct with underage children are not barred from the profession; there is no reliable measure of the extent of sexual violence and harassment in schools; and there is no accountability when schools allowed gender violence to occur unchallenged or concealed instances of abuse.

Fear of Getting Involved

> *The teachers are scared. I can see it, there is a genuine threat to them, it is not a perceived thing. You may have seventeen to nineteen-year-olds with firearms running the school.*

Prosecutor, Durban

> *Everyone is scared for themselves. If you try and take things up you may find yourself in big trouble.*

Teacher, township near Johannesburg

Aside from the absence of guidelines on sexual violence, fear for their own safety may sometimes hinder school officials from responding to student complaints. Violence in schools may pose risks for teachers as well as students.[233] Viewing schools as prime places for recruiting new members and

---

[232] Human Rights Watch interview with vice principal, Cato Manor, April 5, 2000.
[233] Human Rights Watch interview with teacher, Alexandra Township, March 27, 2000; Human Rights Watch interview with teacher, Mitchell's Plain, April 14, 2000; Human Rights Watch interview with teacher, Cape Flats, April 12, 2000.

selling drugs, violent gangs frequently infiltrate schools.[234] Teachers told Human Rights Watch that gang-affiliated students carry weapons to school, challenge school officials, and undermine teachers. Gang-affiliated students may also carry their conflicts with them, posing risks to everyone at school. A Mitchell's Plain teacher told us of the difficulties presented by a student in her class who was believed to be involved in an area gang shooting, "There were rumors that there would be a retaliation hit against [the student], and he sits in my class endangering all the others. I am scared of becoming a casualty."[235] In some areas, teachers are simply afraid for their own safety and fear prevents them from intervening to help their students.

Fear of violent retaliation has stopped one township teacher outside Johannesburg from reporting any student crime to police, after she was personally threatened. She told Human Rights Watch that her school has decided to place the burden of bringing complaints of violence to the police on students: "For us to be safe as individual teachers, the student victim must report the case on her own. I advise kids to go to the police."[236]

Shielding Perpetrators and Concealing Abuse

> *If the abuser is from outside [school], then schools are very supportive, they'll even bring the child in to see us [at Childline counseling center]. But there's a lot of defensiveness if the accused is a teacher, then it becomes the child is lying, or it was a seductive child, or the child wanted it.*
>
> Andrea Engelbrecht, Childline counselor

> *Schools have done nothing about it. Teachers who abuse have been transferred to other schools. Most often, that will happen if anything happens at all to the teacher.*
>
> Rachel Jewkes, Acting Director, Women's Health Research Unit, Medical Research Council

---

[234] Richard Griggs, "School Violence: A Culture of Learning About Drugs, Thugs and Guns," *ChildrenFirst*, February/March 1998, p. 7.

[235] Human Rights Watch interview with teacher, Mitchell's Plain, April 14, 2000.

[236] Human Rights Watch interview with teacher, Alexandra township, March 27, 2000.

VII. The School Response

Despite statutory obligations to report child abuse,[237] when a school employee is accused of committing sexual assault, a common response of school officials is to try to keep the problem within the school community by concealing the existence of abuse and shielding from scrutiny those alleged to have committed acts of sexual violence. Schools often appear to identify criminal conviction as the only point at which an alleged perpetrator should be separated from his victim, through suspension, expulsion, or dismissal from employment. However, in most instances of sexual violence a conviction is not likely.

The case of MC, described above in chapter V, is illustrative. Although MC's parents complained to the school about the teacher, the school failed to contact police and the teacher remained on the job. The principal of MC's school allegedly told her parents not to alert the police to the sexual abuse occurring at the school.[238] MC's mother described her meeting with the school to Human Rights Watch:

> We met with the principal. I told him "my daughter has been raped by one of your teachers." I asked what the school intended to do? What should I do? And I told them I was going to go to the police. The Principal said "don't go to the police until we can talk to the school's lawyer to determine what to do. Don't do anything until we can go to the school board to get this cleared up." He told me "you should not do anything until we talk to the school lawyer, you mustn't go to the CPU [police Child Protection Unit] until the school board can sort out what the school is to do."[239]

---

[237] South African legislation, including the Child Care Act 86 of 1991, as amended, Section 42, establishes mandatory reporting of child abuse. According to the South African Law Commission, although the duty to report initially rested only on medical and dental personnel, the legislature subsequently decided to impose a duty to report on teachers. Pursuant to statutory obligations to report child abuse, any person who examines, treats, attends to, advises, instructs, or cares for a child must report abuse to a police official or child welfare. Failure to comply with statutory reporting requirements constitutes an offense punishable upon conviction by a fine not exceeding R4,000 or imprisonment not exceeding one year or both. Once a report has been made, further action must be taken. South African Law Commission, "Review of the Child Care Act," Issue Paper 13, Project 110 (1998). For further discussion of the statutory obligation to report child abuse see N. Van Dokkum, "The Statutory Obligation to Report Child Abuse and Neglect," in Raylene Keightley (ed.), *Children's Rights* (Kenwyn: Juta and Co., Ltd., 1996).

[238] Human Rights Watch interview with MC's mother, Johannesburg, March 18, 2000.

[239] Ibid.

The school did nothing to sanction the teacher or to help the child. The teacher continued in his teaching duties at the school long after MC's parents confronted the school about the rape, leaving MC and other girls vulnerable to his further abuse.[240] In this instance, because several schools had similarly opted in the past to conceal this teacher's conduct rather than initiate administrative action against him or report him to police, he remained free to go on to different schools and new children, abusing his authority and taking advantage of their trust. The teacher had previously been permitted to resign without censure from another school where he taught, after similar incidents were reported against him.

One counselor, working on the case of a girl who had allegedly been raped by a school caretaker, told Human Rights Watch that generally it is not that school officials do not know what action to take, but rather that "basically schools are covering their butts—schools are being run as businesses. Funding is dependent on enrollment. Bad publicity would be bad. Most teachers have the attitude, 'let's keep away' or 'let's not get involved' or 'it can't be happening at our school.'"[241] She explained her frustrations with what she perceived to be a school's evasiveness in one of her current cases: "I went with the girl's mother to speak with the principal. The principal would not even acknowledge the possibility that the rape had happened, and the medical evidence has shown that an adult sexually abused the child. I told him—'if this man is the perpetrator in this case you are putting other kids at risk.'"[242]

The tendency of schools to shield perpetrators and conceal abuse allegations potentially places numerous children at risk while offering those who have sexually abused students refuge and access to victims within the school system. The mother of TM, an eighteen-year-old student, called Childline in May 1997 to report concerns that a teacher was attempting to sexually abuse TM. She later learned her daughter had not been the teacher's only victim. The student told her mother that on two separate occasions in May, the teacher kissed her and touched her bottom. According to the Childline counselor:

> The teacher had been asking her questions about relationships—whether she has boyfriends. He used to call her father at work to tell him that [the girl] needs private lessons because her performance is so

---

[240] Charlene Smith, "Rape Accused Continues to Teach," *Mail and Guardian,* September 1, 1999.
[241] Human Rights Watch interview with Shamona Reddy, social worker, Johannesburg, March 23, 2000.
[242] Ibid.

VII. The School Response

poor. The parents refused because they didn't like the question that he asks their child.[243]

TM's mother met with the principal and was surprised to learn that the principal already knew of at least two other reported cases.[244] It is far from clear what further evidence this particular principal would have required to take action, if repeated complaints from parents and students were perceived to be insufficient.

Before taking a voluntary leave of absence, a high school teacher in Bishop Lavis continued in his teaching duties for nearly a year after he had allegedly raped DN, a seventeen-year-old student, in an empty school hall in September 1998. DN disclosed the rape to a friend, who told the school guidance counselor, who then reported the rape to the principal. The school took no action against the teacher.[245] A criminal case against the teacher is currently pending.

A Rustenburg teacher remains employed after allegedly raping a student and will likely face no criminal sanction. BG, fifteen, phoned Childline in October 1999 from Rustenburg to talk about her feelings after she was raped by her teacher. The Childline operator summarized the call as follows.

> A year ago the caller was raped by her teacher. She told a female teacher who told the school principal. Parents were also told. Rape charges were filed. School Principal persuaded her mother to drop the charges. Promised to take care of the matter. Nothing has been done yet. Caller finds it difficult to "cope" after the incident. Studies are deteriorating. The teacher still teaches at the same school. Caller never received any counseling. Needs some. Caller sounds very optimistic, but feels disappointed by her mother and school principal.[246]

---

[243] Childline call record, May 1997.
[244] Childline call record, May 1997.
   Called [TM's mother]. She spoke to the principal who revealed that the teacher had done the same thing last year but she couldn't do much because there was not much evidence. Yesterday morning another girl went into his classroom and he kissed her. The girl told the principal.
[245] Human Rights Watch interview with Mallory Issacs, Childline, Bishop Lavis, April 14, 2000.
[246] Childline call record, October 30, 1999.

As in BG's case, school response is often to urge the family to remain silent and not to alert police about abuse with a promise that the matter will be handled internally. Repeatedly, parents told Human Rights Watch that schools asked them not to get the police involved or draw publicity to problems at school. Usually it was publicity and parent protest that prompted any school action. When parents learn that their child has been a victim of violence at school, school officials encourage the parents to deal with the matter within the school, as further demonstrated by LB's case, detailed in chapter V above.

Not only have schools failed to report abuse to police, in some instances schools have failed to alert parents about incidents that occur at school. A prosecutor working on the case of a girl abducted from school by her "boyfriend" told Human Rights Watch how the school failed to alert the child's parents about the abduction:

> I had a case of a schoolgirl with a taxi driver boyfriend. He would abduct the girl from class; she'd be missing for days. On one day that she was abducted her father went to the school and asked, "where is my daughter." He hadn't been called immediately after she'd been taken away, and even after he asked the teachers they told him nothing. It was the other students who finally told him that a man came and took his daughter away.[247]

Failure to Cooperate with Investigators

It is rare that you find schools helping, teachers and principals turn a blind eye. It's like the child is on his or her own. Everyone is scared for themselves. If you try and take things up you may find yourself in big trouble.

Hlengiwe Magwaza, Childline counselor

In our interviews with police, prosecutors, and social workers, schools and the education system were criticized for their roles in facilitating sexual violence by failing to fully cooperate with investigations. One prosecutor said that in her experience:

---

[247] Human Rights Watch interview with Val Melis, Senior Public Prosecutor, Durban, April 3, 2000.

VII. The School Response

> Schools tend to play a standoffish role. They don't want to know about it, especially if it is on their premises—bad publicity. We haven't had any school come forward or teachers trying to help us on any cases when abuse occurs in school.[248]

Police officials made similar observations, saying that schools rarely reported sexual violence in the first instance. The Senior Superintendent Commander of the Family Violence, Child Protection and Sexual Offenses Unit of the South African Police Service observed:

> Most often children report to police directly, by themselves or in the alternative parents will report. Rarely do schools report. Years ago school abuse always stayed within the system, it would wind up in the hands of an educational psychologist, it would have been dealt with in the school system. Schools have a better understanding. There is more openness, but the fact remains that most abuse at school is reported by kids and their parents, not schools.[249]

A prosecutor told Human Rights Watch that in her experience schools could not be relied upon to assist with investigations, particularly where a school employee is the accused:

> I had another case in a preschool of a caretaker who allegedly molested a young girl. There was physical evidence. Her vagina was red, irritated. During the course of the investigation prior to trial, I got a call from the school wanting to discuss the case with me. So I went to the school expecting, perhaps naively, their support. Instead they were positively hostile towards me and aggressively in support of their caretaker. Telling me how he'd worked there for years, he's in his fifties. Basically what it came down to for them was the child was the one with the problem.[250]

A social worker attempting to investigate allegations of sexual abuse against a schoolteacher described the negative experience she had with the school management as follows:

---

[248] Ibid.
[249] Human Rights Watch interview with Anneke Pienaar, Commander: Family Violence, Child Protection and Sexual Offences Unit, Pretoria, March 20, 2000.
[250] Human Rights Watch interview with Val Melis, Senior Public Prosecutor, Durban, April 3, 2000.

Once I approached the Department of Education with a case, asking about a teacher's [an allegedly sexually abusive] work history. They were useless. No record of why he'd resigned from several schools before this latest one. He was never reprimanded or monitored. I'll never call on the Department again. The school wasn't helpful either. The teacher stayed at the school for some time because there were no witnesses to the abuse.[251]

Inappropriate Responses

In the absence of clear guidelines and lacking awareness of how to confront sexual violence, even the most well intentioned teachers may discipline students in ways that are unproductive, sometimes reinforcing violence as a legitimate means of confronting problems.

Human Rights Watch is opposed to the use of corporal punishment against children in schools, however that violence is rationalized.[252] Just as challenging routine domestic violence against women has been a vital part of the advancement of women's rights, challenging physical assaults on children disguised as corrective discipline is vital to improving children's status. Human Rights Watch is encouraged by the national Department of Education's efforts to end the practice of corporal punishment in schools with its recently released guidelines to teachers on alternatives to corporal punishment.[253]

Supporting Victims of Violence

In those instances where schools officials immediately responded to girls who reported abuse, by believing them, seriously investigating allegations, and confronting the attackers in a way that ensured abusive behavior would not remain a threat, girls reported feeling safe and empowered.

For example, when seventeen-year-old NN told her teacher that she had been beaten by a male student from a neighboring school, she was gratified to be believed and supported. The boy had come to NN's school, sought her out, and beat her because she had refused to date him. NN was pleased at her teacher's decisive response:

---

[251] Human Rights Watch interview with Linda Dhabicharam, Childline, Durban, March 29, 2000.
[252] See Human Rights Watch, "Spare the Child: Corporal Punishment in Kenyan Schools," *A Human Rights Watch Report*, vol. 11, no. 6(A), September 1999.
[253] Department of Education, *Alternatives to Corporal Punishment* (Pretoria: Department of Education, October 2000).

VII. The School Response

> I told a teacher and we went to this boy's school together to complain. He is now in jail. He raped another girl and he was caught. I was happy with my school's response. [254]

Although it is not clear whether NN's teacher had much to do with preventing future attacks against NN, she explained that she was happy with the response of her teacher because she received his support. He listened to her and took prompt action on her behalf to protest her attacker's behavior. Sadly, many other girls are not as fortunate.

Experts working on sexual harassment in schools have found most effective those interventions in which school authorities take a proactive stance in confronting sexual violence and harassment, respect the wishes and confidentially of the student victims, and offer the students feedback on how their complaints have been handled.[255] According to experts, most effective are schools that act swiftly and unequivocally to end harassment, offering the target of abuse a variety of options for redress, ranging from an opportunity to confront the offender in a safe and supervised space, to school enforced "stay-a-ways" requiring separation of the victim from the perpetrator for a finite time with teacher oversight and sanctions for violation.

---

[254] Human Rights Watch interview with NN, age seventeen, Durban, April 5, 2000.
[255] See, for example, Stein, *Classrooms and Courtrooms*, pp. 83-94.

VIII. THE CRIMINAL JUSTICE SYSTEM

In two prior reports, Human Rights Watch addressed the role of the South African criminal justice system in responding to the problem of violence against women and girls.[256] We found that South African women victims of violence who seek protection and assistance from the state often encountered unsympathetic or hostile treatment at the hands of police, court clerks, and prosecutors. Frequently, police did not understand the magnitude of the harm of gender violence and the complexity of domestic abuse. Conciliatory approaches were preferred over intervention in even egregious cases of abuse where the perpetrator continued to pose a clear danger to a woman. Often such approaches remove all incentive for women to report violence, as the authorities will take no serious action. Government justice officials' ignorance of the laws designed to protect women's rights also proved problematic. Frequently police corruption and litigation delays and "missing dockets" held up prosecutions of perpetrators.

Reform Efforts

The government has recognized many of these problems and has given a high priority to improving the criminal justice system's response to violence against women and children. Although a detailed review of these reforms is beyond the scope of this report, some noteworthy efforts to improve the response to violence against women and children merit mention. Among the initiatives undertaken have been the creation of specialized "domestic violence, child abuse, and sexual assault" (DCS) units in the police (formerly the Child Protection Units (CPUs)) and specialized family courts that handle many issues surrounding violence in the home.

Law reform is also in process. The South African Law Commission[257] is currently considering revisions to the rape laws to forbid sexual conduct between students and teachers.[258] The commission has published a discussion paper containing proposed changes to South Africa's substantive law of sexual

---

[256]Human Rights Watch, *Violence Against Women in South Africa: State Response to Domestic Violence and Rape* (New York: Human Rights Watch, 1995); Human Rights Watch, *South Africa: Violence Against Women and Medico-Legal System* (New York: Human Rights Watch, 1997).

[257] The South African Law Commission was established by the South African Law Commission Act, No. 19 of 1973. The commission is an advisory body whose aim is the renewal and improvement of the law of South Africa on a continuous basis. The commission conducts research on the laws of the country and makes recommendations for the development, improvement, modernization, and reform of the law.

[258] Human Rights Watch interview with Joan van Niekerk, director of Childline, Durban, April 8, 2000.

VIII. The Criminal Justice System

offenses.[259] The Domestic Violence Act of 1998 overcomes some of the limitations of the prior Prevention of Family Violence Act, by among other things, recognizing marital rape and that abuse can occur in many types of domestic relationships.

In 1995, the same year it ratified CEDAW, South Africa ratified the Convention on the Rights of the Child (CRC) and committed to a range of obligations aimed at establishing and protecting the rights of children, as it had for women. Both the laws and institutions affecting children are in a process of transition.[260] South Africa's National Plan of Action, prepared pursuant to its obligations under CRC, identified the need for the development of a comprehensive juvenile justice system. It is now accepted that children should, as far as possible, not be imprisoned. Under the National Crime Prevention Strategy, one program provides for "secure care" of children accused of committing serious and violent offenses.[261] In practice, however, many hundreds of children are still held in prison due to lack of alternative secure accommodation for those accused or convicted of such offenses.

Courts are working to become "child friendly." Courts now allow "intermediaries" in cases that involve child victims. These volunteers, often attorneys, assist the child in understanding the trial process. Children are permitted to give testimony before the court outside the presence of their alleged abuser.[262]

---

[259] South African Law Commission, "Sexual Offences: The Substantive Law," Discussion Paper 85, Project 107 (1999).

[260] According to the South African Law Commission there are several reasons for the present state of flux including: the new emphasis on children's rights that flow from the Convention on the Rights of the Child; the human rights provisions (including special children's rights enshrined in the constitution); the move away from "Western" legal notions, a result of the recognition of different cultural and religious interests in South African society; and increasing political awareness of the needs of children in especially difficult circumstances. The present South African position on legal rules affecting children involves a blend of Roman-Dutch principles, comprising the case law body of rules generally known as the law of parent and child, together with numerous statutory provisions—chief among them the Child Care Act. For discussions of the status of children under South African law, see, generally, J.C. Becker, *The Law of Children and Young Persons in South Africa* (1997); Raylene Keightley (ed.), *Children's Rights* (Kenwyn: Juta and Co., Ltd, 1996); Philip Alston, Stephen Parker, and John Seymour (eds.), *Children, Rights, and the Law* (1992).

[261] South African Law Commission, "Review of the Child Care Act," Issue Paper 13, Project 110 (1998).

[262] A child's ability to testify in court is not linked to a specific age limit, and depends on the child's maturity and understanding of what it means to tell the truth. However, the

Innovations in management of juvenile offenders are occurring as well. Prosecutors are increasingly using "diversion" with young offenders, that is diverting them from incarceration.[263] Prosecuting authorities identify cases for diversion based on factors such as the age of the perpetrator, whether the perpetrator has a fixed residence, whether supervisory authority can be exercised over him, and the severity of the crime committed.[264] Where appropriate, the prosecutor's office will enter into a contract with the perpetrators and their guardians, requiring the perpetrator to receive counseling for three years. A perpetrator who fails to comply risks prosecution, but otherwise if the perpetrator complies there is no criminal record.[265]

Human Rights Watch believes criminalization should not be the sole response to the phenomenon of school violence; in particular, where the perpetrator is a child the education and justice systems should devise responses aimed at preventing future abusive behavior and assisting the victims. In a criminal justice system where convictions for rape and sexual abuse are low, we are in accord with South African children's rights advocates in supporting diversion as a means to monitor, supervise, and rehabilitate juvenile offenders.

Response of the Criminal Justice System to Gender Violence in Schools

Coordination between the education and justice systems on investigating cases of sexual violence to ensure punishment of perpetrators is often ineffective, ill-conceived, or nonexistent. Despite legal obligations to bring sexual abuse to the attention of police, schools frequently fail to do so. Police officials confirmed that in most instances the child and family report sexual abuse that occurs at school; rarely do schools report the crime. Prosecutors express concern that schools are not fully cooperative with investigations of sexual abuse. One Pretoria area prosecutor told Human Rights Watch that, in

---

"cautionary rule" of evidence applies to children's testimony, which requires additional corroboration. Some South African child abuse experts have argued this rule has an unjustified discriminatory effect against children. See P.J. Schwikkard, "The Abused Child: A Few Rules of Evidence Considered," in Raylene Keightley (ed.), *Children's Rights* (Kenwyn: Juta and Co., Ltd, 1996), p. 154.

[263] Human Rights Watch interview with Thoko Majokweni, Special Director, Sexual Offence and Community Affairs Unit, National Prosecuting Authority of South Africa, Pretoria, March 22, 2000.

[264] Ibid.

[265] Human Rights Watch interview with Val Melis, Senior Public Prosecutor, Durban, April 3, 2000.

VIII. The Criminal Justice System

her experience, "the department of education doesn't interact at all, and we need to establish that link."[266]

In addition, the two systems are sometimes confused about their roles. Young perpetrators provide a real conundrum for the education and justice systems. Schools refuse to address accusations of rape through the school disciplinary process on the ground that it is a police matter. If the accused is young, police do not seek criminal penalties. Often, the young accused and the victim will continue to attend the same school:

> I had a case of a girl attending a township school; she was nine when she was raped in the school toilets by a ten-year-old perpetrator. He is still at school. Childline has been trying to work with both children. The School has not suspended the child, on the ground that the matter has been turned over to police, but the police aren't pursing the case because the perpetrator is too young. Both children are still at the same school. Childline is actually counseling the girl on how to cope with running into him at school. The mother of the girl is very upset, but her parents don't have money to send her to another school.[267]

Many instances of sexual violence and rape occurring in schools never reach the criminal justice system. Police and prosecutors maintain that the justice system does not see many school violence cases because often the cases do not get to that point.

Informal dispute settlements and "seduction damage" payments are used to resolve some rape cases outside the criminal justice system. Parents opt to settle the matter out of court, particularly where a child is responsible for an act of sexual violence. Frequently, however, informal settlements do not deter future abuse or provide the victim needed assistance.

As with cases involving adult women, there is often a disturbing willingness on the part of police to dismiss sexual abuse if a girl has an ongoing

---

[266] Human Rights Watch interview with Thoko Majokweni, Prosecutor, Pretoria, March 22, 2000.
[267] Human Rights Watch interview with Hlengiwe Magwaza, Childline, Durban, March 28, 2000.

relationship, of whatever kind, with the accused. For example, in one case, criminal charges were dropped against a teacher from the West Rand after the sixteen-year-old he was accused of raping said she consented to a relationship with him.[268]

---

[268] "Teacher Quits in Disgrace," *Sowetan*, March 16, 2000.

IX. NATIONAL AND PROVINCIAL GOVERNMENT RESPONSE

We have a lot of sexual violence in schools; we don't have a strategy. People are working on it, but not in a coordinated way.

Gender Focal Person, Western Cape Education Department

The incidence of sexual violence and harassment in schools has remained largely unchronicled in South Africa. Although there are no reliable statistics on the extent of sexual violence experienced by girls in South African schools, the government has recognized the problem as a serious one. A Gender Equity Task Team (GETT), commissioned in 1996 by the Department of Education to analyze the education system from a gender perspective, identified the problem of sexual violence in schools as severe and systemic, and raised concerns about the perceived levels of violence against South African schoolgirls.

In its 1997 report, *Gender Equity in Education*, the GETT observed, "[w]hat is not necessarily fully acknowledged is the extent of rape in schools, and on the way to and from schools."[269] The GETT report noted that while violence and harassment had been documented in the behavior of teachers, and students towards other students, there was not sufficient data about the prevalence of violence in schools or who the perpetrators were. South African children's rights activists assert that sexual abuse in schools is widespread. Childline, a nongovernmental organization assisting victims of child abuse, has estimated that one in three South African girls under the age of sixteen will be sexually abused.[270] Often the abuse will occur at school.

The South African government has acknowledged unacceptably high levels of sexual violence and harassment in its schools and has expressed a commitment at the highest policy making levels to addressing violence in schools and against girls at school.[271] There are national and provincial initiatives on various aspects of school violence under development or being implemented. Curriculum components on gender equity are being devised. Although the national Department of Education has indicated a desire to develop

---

[269] Wolpe, *Gender Equity in Education*, p. 94.
[270] Human Rights Watch interview with Lynn Cawood, director of Childline-Gauteng, Johannesburg, March 14, 2000.
[271] See Charlene Smith, "Asmal: School Rape a National Crisis," *Mail and Guardian*, October 15, 1999, quoting Minister of Education Kader Asmal as stating: "Sexual violence in schools must be rooted out and I will take a personal interest in this happening."

a comprehensive policy on sexual violence and harassment in schools,[272] there is as yet no national policy and the implementation and enforcement of existing protections has not been rigorous. In addition, the necessary coordination between the education and justice systems required to address the problem effectively constantly falters.

The Gender Equity Task Team called on the national Department of Education to develop a schools policy and standard procedure for intervention in child abuse, and to establish expectations that schools provide easily accessible information on and referral to services and resources that support the needs of children. The Task Team also urged enactment of legislation allocating clear responsibility to all educational managers for ensuring a discrimination- and violence-free environment.

The Task Team also urged the national and provincial education departments to "develop guidelines and accountability frameworks for addressing violence....as an integral part of the school quality assurance process." The team suggested that the national and provincial departments work to "position issues pertaining to the safety and security of girls in legal frameworks in order to locate responsibility to the perpetrators of violence."[273]

On the provincial level, the team recommended that professional development and teaching material be developed for school governing boards and teachers on the nature of sex-based and ethnic violence. It suggested that awareness programs for parents and communities on gender violence should be promoted in conjunction with these other efforts.

While all of the Task Team recommendations have not been fully integrated into policies across the education system, the national Department of Education has designed general school violence initiatives that should benefit all children. Certain provincial education departments in cooperation with nongovernmental organizations are engaged in school-based interventions to assist children to cope with and combat school violence. The Western Cape department, for example, has drafted a specific gender violence policy that holds promise as a model for improving the system's response to violence against girls. These initiatives, described briefly below, will require cooperation and coordination among all stakeholders in the education system for their effective implementation.[274] In many cases it is too early to evaluate the efficacy of these

---

[272] Human Rights Watch telephone interview with Bheki Khumalo, liaison to the Minister of Education, December 6, 2000.
[273] Wolpe, *Gender Equity*, p. 110.
[274] For current research on school violence and anti-crime initiatives in South African schools, see, generally, Phillip Bongani, *Violence in South African Township Schools: An Exploration* (Cape Town: Institute of Criminology, UCT, 1999); Cheryl Frank and Ninnette Eliasov, *Crime and Violence in Schools: An Exploratory Study into the*

IX. National and Provincial Government Response

initiatives, but early efforts are encouraging. A greater expansion of the programs described below as well as enforcement of existing laws would enhance system-wide efforts to prevent, investigate, and punish sexual violence in schools.

Legal Reforms

In 2000, the South African parliament amended the 1998 Employment of Educators Act to expand the scope of actions considered "serious misconduct" and to include a disciplinary code and procedure for employers to use when it is alleged that a teacher has committed misconduct.[275] Now committing an act of sexual assault on a student or having a sexual relationship with a student constitutes serious misconduct that warrants dismissal if an educator is found guilty of the offense. The act details the sanctions that may be imposed and describes how an employer should conduct disciplinary hearings in cases of misconduct.[276]

The 1996 South African Schools Act provides for the suspension of pupils as a "correction measure," or their expulsion for "serious misconduct" after a fair hearing. It is left to each provincial MEC responsible for education to "determine by notice" the behavior which may constitute serious misconduct and the disciplinary procedure to be followed.[277]

Experiences of Crime and Violence in Schools in Transition (Cape Town: Institute of Criminology, 1998); *Need Analysis of Conditions in Schools* (Cape Town: Trauma Center for Survivors of Violence and Torture, 1999); G. Wyngaard, et al., *A Comparative Study on Primary and Secondary School Learners' Perceptions of Safety, Injury and Violence in Seven Schools in a Peri-Urban Setting in the Western Cape Region of South Africa* (Cape Town: University of South Africa, 1999); *Anti-Crime Initiatives in Selected Schools in the Cape Town Metropolitan Area and West Coast* (Cape Town: Early Learning Resource Unity and Quaker Peace Centre, 1999); Sarah Henkeman, et al, *Evaluation of Impact of the Electric Fence at Manenberg Secondary School* (Cape Town: Resources Unlimited, 1999).

[275]Education Laws Amendment Act, No. 53 of 2000, Section 17. The act amends the Employment of Educators Act, No. 76 of 1998, to provide that an educator must be dismissed if he or she is found guilty of, among other things: "committing an act of sexual assault on a learner, student or other employee"; "having a sexual relationship with a learner of the school where he or she is employed"; or "seriously assaulting, with the intention to cause grievous bodily harm to, a learner, student or other employee." The section further provides that "If it is alleged that an educator committed a serious misconduct conduct contemplated in subsection (1), the employer must institute disciplinary proceedings."

[276]Education Laws Amendment Act, No. 53 of 2000, Schedule 2.

[277] South African Schools Act, No. 84 of 1996, section 9.

Guidelines on HIV/AIDS

The education department in South Africa also recently recognized the problem of teachers sexually abusing female students in its warning against sexual misconduct in new school guidelines on HIV/AIDS issues.[278] The guidelines note the prevalence of the problem and call on teachers to refrain from sex with students because of the dangers of HIV transmission and because "having sex with learners betrays the trust of the community."[279] The HIV/AIDS guidelines explain that sexual relations between teachers and students are illegal:

> *Educators must not have sexual relations with learners. It is against the law, even if the learner consents. Such action transgresses the code of conduct for educators, who are in a position of trust.
> *Strict disciplinary action will be taken against any educator who has sex with a learner.
> *Sex that is demanded by an educator without consent is rape, which is a serious crime, and the educator will be charged. If an educator has sex with a girl or boy who is under 16 years, he or she will be charged with statutory rape and may face a penalty of life imprisonment.
> *If you are aware of a colleague who is having sexual relations with a learner you must report them to the principal or higher educational authorities, and if the boy or girl is under 16, to the police. If you do not do so you may be charged with being an accessory to rape.[280]

The guidelines also offer educators basic facts about HIV/AIDS and key messages about preventing HIV infection. Educators are urged to teach children about HIV/AIDS. Further, educators are instructed on how to prevent disease transmission in schools, how to manage accidents and injuries, and how to reduce the risk of transmitting illness to people with HIV/AIDS. The guidelines advise educators to build an enabling environment and culture of

---

[278] In response to the high prevalence of HIV/AIDS in South Africa, particularly among youth, the Department of Education developed a national policy on HIV/AIDS for students and teachers in public schools. The policy seeks to promote effective prevention and care within the public education system and focuses on providing accurate information on: the nature and risk factors of HIV infection and AIDS; precautionary measures; and the obligation resting on school communities to avoid discrimination against infected persons. Rachel Jewkes, *The HIV/AIDS Emergency: Department of Education Guidelines for Educators* (Pretoria: Department of Education, 2000).
[279] Jewkes, *The HIV/AIDS Emergency*.
[280] Ibid.

nondiscrimination for those students and teachers living with HIV/AIDS. The guidelines encourage schools to develop their own policies on HIV/AIDS in order to give effect to these national guidelines.

National Initiatives on School Violence

In July 1999, Education Minister Asmal issued a call to action and statement of priorities for the revitalization of South Africa's education system. His pronouncement presented a vision of educational transformation, and prioritized areas of the education system requiring urgent attention. The minister emphasized the importance of turning schools into centers of community life by combating violence in schools.[281] The department has also identified upgrading the qualifications of the country's teachers as a major priority to focus primarily on farm and rural schools. The department has developed a plan for interim teacher qualifications and a national professional diploma in education registered with the South African Qualifications Authority.[282]

In 1999, the department also launched "Tirisano" (working together), a nine-point plan of action to be implemented over five years with the broad aim of repairing the South African school system. Tirisano has a school safety component aimed at ensuring that all schools are free from crime, violence, and sexual harassment.[283] The department is now in the process of collaborating with the Secretariat for Safety and Security and the National Youth Commission to develop a Joint Framework Document on strategies to address youth violence in schools as a part of Tirisano.[284] The framework document outlines a multi-departmental intervention strategy to address youth violence within certain targeted schools. The proposed intervention strategies are designed to mobilize and integrate multiple levels and sectors of government and civil society. The document marks the culmination of the first phase of development. The violence reduction strategy calls on all stakeholders to address the social system

---

[281] Shireen Motala, Salim Vally, and Maropeng Modiba, "A Call to Action: A Review of Minister K. Asmal's Educational Priorities," *Quarterly Review of Education and Training in South Africa*, vol. 6, no. 3 (September 1999).
[282] "Asmal: South Africa Has Thousands of Unqualified or Under-Qualified Teachers," *Mail and Guardian*, December 8, 2000.
[283] Letter from M.T. Mokhobo, Director Gender Equity, National Department of Education, to Human Rights Watch, January 24, 2001.
[284] Human Rights Watch interview with Margaret Roper, Johannesburg, March 19, 2000; Porteus, *Tirisano: Towards an Intervention Strategy to Address Youth Violence in Schools*.

underlying youth violence, to eliminate spaces for violence, and to facilitate learning.

Since 1997, when it launched the Campaign for a Culture of Learning, Teaching and Service (COLTS), the government has worked to create school-based programs to aid in transforming South African schools from sites of struggle to places of "learning, teaching and service."[285] The COLTS "No Crime in Schools" Component aims to counter the undermining effects of hostile school environments to learning. This component is part of the National Crime Prevention Strategy (NCPS), an interdepartmental strategy created in May 1995, as part of the Government of National Unity's recognition of high levels of crime in society. NCPS has three prongs in its implementation strategy involving schools: school safety, violence prevention, and victim empowerment through the "Life Skills" curriculum.

More recently, the department has released an interactive manual for teachers on alternatives to corporal punishment. The document suggests ways in which teachers can be proactive and set up the learning environment to limit discipline problems and suggests strategies to use.[286] Human Rights Watch is encouraged by the government's commitment to end corporal punishment as well as its efforts to address the problem through prohibiting the practice, educating educators on alternatives to violence, and requesting that charges be laid against abusive teachers. Human Rights Watch is hopeful that the department will confront sexual violence in schools with similar urgency.

National Initiatives on Gender Equity

The National Department of Education has also established a Directorate for Gender Equity, based on the 1997 recommendations of the Gender Equity Task Team, in order to mainstream gender equity in all aspects of the education

---

[285] Linda Biersteker, *Baseline Study of Research Done on Anti-Crime Initiatives at School Level* (COLTS, 2000).

[286] Launching the manual, the minister of education stated:
> Despite its prohibition, we are aware of continuing cases of corporal punishment, which are brought to our attention, or reported in the media. We have to be firm and in some cases we have requested that charges be laid against the educator concerned. But we also have a responsibility to assist teachers to manage without the cane, which for many teachers over many years has been the only way of administering discipline in schools. Fear of being hit might induce a learner to sit still and be quite for a while, but it cannot be a basis for effective learning. And we do not want a cowering child to emerge from our schools; we want confident, affirmed youths, ready to take on the world.

Kader Asmal, press conference, Cape Town, available at http://education.pwv.gov.za/Media/Speeches_2000/October00/Corporal_Punishment.htm, Cape Town, October 5, 2000 (accessed February 13, 2001).

IX. National and Provincial Government Response

system and to work closely with provincial departments. Recently, provincial gender equity units were created. Each province has now identified a "gender focal person" to head these units, though no clear mandate has been given to them beyond a responsibility to study and advise on all aspects of gender equity in education.[287] Human Rights Watch believes gender violence in schools should be a high priority of the provincial directorates.

Human Rights Watch interviewed gender focal persons leading the gender equity units from four of the country's nine provinces and learned that, unfortunately, the gender focal persons were not a high priority of provincial directorates. Gender focal persons told us that their posts were not at the director or even deputy director level within their respective provincial departments of education.[288] Gender focal persons told us that they were rarely, if ever, included in important meetings of the department where policies are being set and decisions made—which they attributed to occupying rather low level posts within provincial education departments. For instance, gender focal persons told us that the national Department of Education had as yet failed to develop a policy or comprehensive strategy to address gender violence. Nor had the department consulted them about designing procedural guidelines for schools on how to address sexual violence and harassment. All believed that gender issues were sufficiently important and the problems sufficiently urgent to merit their input and consultation in policy making.

The Gender Equity Task Team called for each provincial department of education to have a gender equity unit and a gender director. Gender equity focal persons told us that they did not have a unit, but rather that one person without staff or resources usually takes on additional responsibilities for addressing all gender equity problems in schools for the provincial education administration. One gender focal person told Human Rights Watch that her post was merely an "add on" on top of her many other work responsibilities so that in practice she could devote little time to sexual violence problems in the schools of her province.

---

[287] Ansuyah Maharaj, "Provinces Quick-Pic Gender Focal Desks," *Agenda,* no. 41, 1999. According to South African women's groups, "[n]o clear mandate was given to the provincial GEUs. Their role was summarized by the GETT report as to 'study and advise' the Director-General on all aspects of gender equity in the education system." Ibid.

[288] The GETT report called for each provincial department of education to have a gender equity unit and a gender director. The report recommended that each provincial gender equity unity be located at the highest level of the provincial administration system and attached to the office of the head of department. Wolpe, *Gender Equity in Education*, pp. 12-14.

Despite these challenges, gender focal persons have been active in efforts to develop mechanisms for schools to address gender violence.[289] In November 1999, under the auspices of the Canada-South Africa Education Management Program (CSAEMP), a joint initiative of the Canadian International Development Agency, the national Department of Education, and McGill University (Montreal), a team of gender focal persons began working to develop an education module for school management on sex-based and gender-based violence. The module outlines a series of workshops on the issues for gender and sexual violence, sexual harassment, child abuse, and strategies for dealing with student disclosures. The module also explains the need for schools to develop sexual harassment policies as a way to protect against legal actions and create a positive school environment.[290] It is of urgent importance that this forthcoming school-based educational module be widely disseminated to schools. Human Rights Watch expects that such instructional materials can be valuable tools for increasing awareness about the existence and harm of sexual violence and harassment in schools and encourages support for such initiatives at every level within the education system.

Human Rights Watch urges the education system to support gender focal persons and gender equity units in their efforts to address sexual violence in schools. Human Rights Watch encourages the education system to provide resources and support to gender focal persons and to consider elevating the status of gender equity units within the administrative structure of education in order to better facilitate their input into education policy.

Provincial Initiatives

The Western Cape Education Department has drafted a procedure to deal with complaints of sexual harassment and child abuse by students, educators, and school employees that is currently under review.[291] The primary objective of the policy is to provide a procedure whereby a student can lodge a complaint if he or she has been sexually harassed or abused by another student, an educator, or another department employee. The draft provides for the creation of an environment where it is easy for a student to report misconduct by

---

[289] For a survey of recent initiatives and the challenges of implementation see Olly Mlamleli, Pontsho Mabelane, Vernet Napo, Ntombi Sibiya, and Valerie Free, "Creating Programs for Safe Schools: Opportunities and Challenges in Relation to Gender-Based Violence in South Africa," in *McGill Journal of Education*, vol. 35, no. 3 (Fall 2000).

[290] Human Rights Watch interview with Claudia Mitchell, Gender Equity Coordinator for the Canada-South Africa Education Sector Management Program, Montreal, January 15, 2001.

[291] Human Rights Watch interview with Beverly Berry, Gender Equity Focal Person, Western Cape Education Department, Cape Town, April 12, 2000.

ensuring confidentiality. The department expects that the new procedures will soon enable administrators to deal swiftly and adequately with sexual misconduct in area schools.[292] The draft also contemplates provision of support systems for students who are victims of abuse by setting up a referral system to other service providers. Potential sanctions for offenders are not outlined in the draft policy.[293]

Initiatives of Professional Associations

The South African Council for Educators has distributed a framework of professional ethics for teachers calling upon educators to refrain from any form of sexual relationship with students or sexual harassment, physical or otherwise.[294] The council, mandated by the South African Council of Educators Act 31 of 2000, is an educators' professional licensing and disciplinary body with which the government now requires all South African teachers to register.

The council recently announced that it intends to launch a national investigation into the extent of sexual harassment and abuse of pupils by teachers.[295] According to the council, the investigation was prompted by problems encountered with victims and witnesses withdrawing from sexual abuse cases against teachers. Human Rights Watch welcomes the council's investigation and hopes any findings will be used to contribute to the development of a comprehensive strategy to end sexual violence and harassment in schools. Human Rights Watch also hopes that findings in this report and others will assist the National Department of Education to be more effective in its own efforts to address the problem of sexual violence and harassment in schools.

Nongovernmental Partnership Projects

Education departments have accepted offers of assistance from NGO partners positively and with great benefit to children. A small but exciting school violence initiative, the Crime Reduction in Schools Project (CRISP), is underway in a few schools in KwaZulu-Natal. CRISP, based in the Office of

---

[292] Western Cape Education Department, "Proposed Gender-based Violence Manual for WCED Employees and Procedures Applicable to the Western Cape Education Department in Dealing with Complaints of Sexual Harassment or Abuse by Learners, Educators, and Employees," (January 2000).

[293] Ibid. It should be noted that the Western Cape is the best funded department with the highest per capita expenditure for its students.

[294] South African Council for Educators Code of Conduct (2000). See Appendix C.

[295] Moshoeshoe Monare, "Sex Harassment by Teachers Under Spotlight," *Star*, January 14, 2001.

Community Out Service Learning at the University of Natal, Durban, is a comprehensive multi-disciplinary intervention and research program aimed at crime prevention in schools. Supported primarily by the South African Department of Arts, Culture, Science and Technology's Innovation Fund, the CRISP program is a pilot project in six Durban area schools, which has as its focus the development of a holistic model for crime prevention.[296]

Through CRISP, university students and community partners are working together to provide a range of programs in schools including: group and individual counseling services to help students, teachers, and parents; diversity training to increase understanding and tolerance of racial and gender differences; environment management to assess the learning environment and school infrastructure and review its impact on students; and policy implementation and evaluation. Girls attending schools participating in CRISP that we interviewed spoke highly of the individual counselors assigned to their schools and appreciated the assistance. School-based counseling was important for many girls who did not have resources or transportation to seek assistance elsewhere. Also in KwaZulu-Natal, the Independent Projects Trust investigated ten Durban schools to identify the sources and conditions promoting school violence to identify sources and conditions promoting violence in area schools and possible ways to address the problem.[297]

In Gauteng, the Centre for the Study of Violence and Reconciliation has been working with the Soweto Safe Schools project since 1994 to help students and teachers in Soweto to cope with the aftermath of years of political violence. Educators are being trained to deal with trauma in forty area schools. Teacher committees in these schools have helped to direct the project and increasing emphasis has been given to the issues of HIV/AIDS and sexual harassment.[298]

The Nelson Mandela Children's Fund, an independent trust formed by South Africa's first democratically elected president, is active in forming partnerships among organizations working directly with children, and has sponsored the development of a guide on the effective management of sexual abuse. The manual has been designed to assist educators in handling situations where they either suspect that a student has been sexually abused or when the student discloses abuse. The manual proposes elements that a school policy regarding child abuse should contain and sets out a referral procedure. Some

---

[296] Human Rights Watch interview with Colin AJ Collett van Rooyen, CRISP, Durban, March 31, 2000.
[297] Human Rights Watch interview with Val Smith, IPT, Durban, March 29, 2000.
[298] Human Rights Watch interview with Dorothy Mdluli, Manager, Youth Department, Centre for the Study of Violence and Reconciliation, Johannesburg, March 14, 2000; Linda Biersteker, *Baseline Study of Research Done on Anti-Crime Initiatives at School Level* (COLTS, 2000).

IX. National and Provincial Government Response

teachers are now being trained on sexual abuse. Distributed primarily in Gauteng, many area teachers are nevertheless not aware of the existence of the manual. Again, greater dissemination of this important information is essential.

Another nongovernmental organization, the South African chapter of the Forum for African Women Educationalists (FAWE), in collaboration with the Western Cape and Gauteng Departments of Education, in 1998 assessed the work being done on sexual harassment and discussed ideas for an action project on sexual harassment in secondary schools. FAWE identified many of the problems associated with sexual harassment in South African schools and further work is needed to follow up.

These initiatives, while in early stages, are the start of collaboration among provincial departments of education and nongovernmental organizations to end gender violence in schools. Although there are a growing number of initiatives, there is, to date, no coordinated strategy to address the problem of sexual violence in South African schools in a systemic fashion.

Challenges Ahead

With proper implementation and expansion across the country, the efforts described above should, taken together, yield improved safety conditions for South African children. However, government efforts to prevent, punish, and remedy sexual violence against schoolgirls must be further strengthened. The South African government faces immense and complex challenges in addressing the legacy of apartheid in many aspects of government, yet the following initiatives could and should be implemented without excessive cost.

- *Identification and Tracking of Abusive Teachers*

Currently there is no legislation that prohibits provincial departments from hiring staff who have been convicted on criminal charges of sex crimes. There is also no requirement that schools gather and pass on information about teachers who are fired or transferred as a result of their sexual abuse or harassment of students. Schools do not have easy access to the names and identities of individuals who pose a risk to children. Therefore, it is difficult for schools to screen out employment applicants who may pose a danger to children. The problem of sexual violence against girls by teachers is sufficiently serious that schools should be required to pass on such information about individuals who present a danger to children.

Efforts to improve the school system's response to sexual violence would be greatly enhanced by reliable data detailing the nature and degree of such violence in schools. Presently, there is no quantitative information official or unofficial figures documenting the full scope of the problem. As the school system has no data collection procedure concerning crimes of sexual violence at school, crafting interventions to prevent and remedy abuse is more difficult.

- **Reporting Mechanisms**

Problems in reporting may be alleviated by establishing mechanisms that allow children to report abuse safe from hostility and humiliation. Students do not have secure places to lodge complaints of sexual violence to school authorities. At present, children typically approach a trusted teacher and disclose abuse. The allegation may or may not be acted upon. Independent investigations of abuse allegations in schools would serve to protect the confidentiality of children as well as the due process rights of the alleged abuser. As the situation stands, investigations are not uniform, and even within the same school, similar complaints are treated differently by school authorities.

The education and justice systems do little to hold the schools accountable for their failure to alert relevant authorities about abuse or credible allegations that abuse was perpetrated by members of the school community. Despite laws that require educators to disclose abuse, Human Rights Watch was not able to find a single case of a school or teacher having faced the criminal sanctions called for by South African law for either failing to alert relevant authorities to or for concealing sexual abuse within the school community. These laws should be publicized and enforced.

- **Protection for Complainants**

The education system does little to redress the harms schoolgirls subjected to sexual violence suffer. There is little protection for a child complainant's privacy. There is often no support structure designed to assist victims of sexual violence. No policies are in place providing guidance to schools as to what alternative schooling should be given to girls who fear attending courses with their abusers are in place. The school system has no mechanism to provide for the education of girls who leave their schools out of fear of sexual violence or after experiencing sexual abuse.

Although sexual violence and abuse happens at school, the services and responses contemplated by many of the draft policies are geared towards abuse by strangers and do not address girls' needs for justice and safety at school. In the design of many of the violence reduction initiatives, the focus has been on violence in black and township schools, but violence is by no means unique to them. Violence such as corporal punishment, assaults, bullying, rape, and sexual and emotional abuse among students and between teachers is widespread and exists in some exclusive schools. We found girls from all levels of society and among all ethnic groups that had been affected by various forms of sexual violence and harassment at school. A system-wide response is urgently needed.

IX. National and Provincial Government Response

- ***Coordination and Communication of Policies***

Currently, policy coordination is lacking and communication gaps are common between the national and provincial education departments and schools. For instance, the minister of education's guidelines on HIV/AIDS for the school system have been met with resistance at the local level in some areas. Individual schools fail to implement policies, while relevant policies have yet to be implemented consistently across government departments. One provincial education department official expressed her concern over the breakdown in control over schools as follows:

> As much as we develop policy, nothing will happen if schools aren't held accountable. Individual school principals must be held accountable. By the time a policy gets to the school nobody is accountable. We need them to access information and policies meant to deal with school problems and we must be able to hold schools accountable for certain things that happen at school.[299]

---

[299] Human Rights Watch interview with Beverley Barry, Gender Focal Person, Cape Town, April 12, 2000.

X. SOUTH AFRICA'S OBLIGATIONS UNDER INTERNATIONAL AND NATIONAL LAW

International Law

International law requires states to address persistent violations of human rights and take measures to prevent their occurrence. With respect to violations of bodily integrity, states have a duty to prosecute abuse, whether the violation is committed by an agent of the state or a private citizen.[300] When states routinely fail to respond to evidence of rape or sexual assault of women and girls, they send the message that such attacks can be committed with impunity.[301] In so doing, states fail to take the minimum steps necessary to protect the right of women and girls to physical integrity or even life.[302] When a state tolerates violations of the bodily integrity of female students in educational settings, it allows gender-based violence to erect a discriminatory barrier to the ability of female students to enjoy their right to education.

Sexual Violence as Discrimination

International law requires South Africa to ensure that women are able to enjoy basic human rights and fundamental freedoms on an equal basis with men.[303] Through its 1995 ratification of the U.N. Convention on the Elimination of All Forms of Discrimination Against Women (CEDAW), South Africa has assumed the obligation to "pursue by all appropriate means and without delay a

---

[300] Article 2 of the International Covenant on Civil and Political Rights (ICCPR) requires governments to provide an effective remedy for abuses and to ensure the rights to life and security of the person of all individuals in their jurisdiction, without distinction of any kind including sex. Article 3 of the ICCPR provides: "The States Parties to the present Covenant undertake to ensure the equal right of men and women to the enjoyment of all civil and political rights set forth in the present Covenant." Article 6 of the ICCPR provides, in pertinent part, that: "Every human being has the inherent right to life. This right shall be protected by law. No one shall be arbitrarily deprived of his life." Article 9 of the ICCPR provides, in pertinent part, that: "Everyone has the right to liberty and security of person."

[301] For a more detailed discussion of South Africa's obligations under international law, see Human Rights Watch, *Violence Against Women in South Africa*, pp. 39-43.

[302] To the extent that this failure reflects discrimination on the basis of gender and/or race, it also constitutes a violation of the state's international obligation to guarantee equal protection of the law.

[303] CEDAW generally prohibits discrimination against women by making impermissible "any distinction, exclusion or restriction made on the basis of sex which has the effect or purpose of impairing or nullifying the recognition, enjoyment or exercise by women. . . on a basis of equality of men and women, of human rights and fundamental freedoms in the political, economic, social, cultural, civil or any other field."

X. South Africa's Obligations Under International and National Law 107

policy of eliminating discrimination against women 'by refraining' from engaging in any act or practice of discrimination against women."[304] To this end South Africa must ensure that public authorities and institutions act in conformity with the obligation not to discriminate against women, including by adopting legislative or other measures to prohibit discrimination, and by ensuring through competent national tribunals and other public institutions the effective protection of women against any act of discrimination.[305]

The U.N. Committee on the Elimination of Discrimination Against Women, established under CEDAW, has noted that "gender-based violence is a form of discrimination which seriously inhibits women's ability to enjoy rights and freedoms on a basis of equality with men." The committee also stated that the general prohibition of gender discrimination includes gender-based violence. Gender-based violence is violence that is directed against a woman because she is a woman, or which affects women disproportionately. Gender-based violence includes acts that inflict physical, mental, or sexual harm or suffering, threats of such acts, coercion, or other deprivations of liberty.[306] Similarly, article 34 of

---

[304] CEDAW, art. 2(d).

[305] Article 4 of the Declaration on the Elimination of Violence Against Women, adopted by the U.N. General Assembly in 1994, calls on states to "pursue by all appropriate means and without delay a policy of eliminating violence against women" and, among other things, to "exercise due diligence to prevent, investigate and in accordance with national legislation, punish acts of violence against women, whether those acts are perpetrated by the State or by private persons." Declaration on the Elimination of Violence Against Women, GAOR, 48th Sess., U.N. Document A/Res/48/104/1994, February 23, 1994. A U.N. declaration is a non-binding resolution which sets out a common international standard that states should follow.

[306] Article 1 of the Declaration on the Elimination of Violence Against Women defines violence against women as "any act of gender-based violence that results in, or is likely to result in, physical, sexual or psychological harm or suffering to women, including threats of such acts, coercion or arbitrary deprivation of liberty, whether occurring in public or private life." Pursuant to Article 2 of the Declaration, the definition further includes, but is not limited to:

a. Physical, sexual and psychological violence occurring in the family, including battering, sexual abuse of female children in the household, dowry-related violence, martial rape, female genital mutilation and other traditional practices harmful to women, non-spousal violence and violence related to exploitation;

b. Physical, sexual and psychological violence occurring within the general community, including rape, sexual abuse, sexual harassment and intimidation at work, in education institutions and elsewhere, trafficking in women and forced prostitution.

c. Physical, sexual and psychological violence perpetrated or condoned by the State, wherever it occurs.

the Convention on the Rights of the Child requires state parties to undertake to protect the child from all forms of sexual exploitation and sexual abuse.

As illustrated through their testimonies, many South African girls have suffered great harm at the hands of their male teachers and classmates. The remedies available to them are usually inadequate or nonexistent. Sexual violence is a form of gender discrimination, and South Africa is obligated to take all appropriate measures to eliminate violence against girls as against women more generally. This is especially true where teachers, who are government agents, are implicated. The government has an obligation to take meaningful steps to prevent teachers from committing acts of violence against students, and to investigate and prosecute teachers who commit acts of violence against school children. Schools, as public institutions, are responsible for reporting crimes committed against students. Furthermore, the systematic failure of the state to hold students accountable for acts of violence against their classmates is itself a violation of human rights law.

The obligations enumerated by the CEDAW Committee extend beyond the justice system and encompass preventive and protective measures including counseling and support services. [307] This would include provision of medical and psychological assistance to girls who are victims of violence. Also in line with these principles would be the provision of medical assistance to victims of sexual violence consistent with the prevailing best practice on post HIV/AIDS-exposure prophylaxis to decrease the likelihood of contracting the virus.

The Right to Nondiscriminatory Education

Education is recognized internationally as a fundamental right for all children. Moreover, a state that provides an education system for children cannot provide schooling in a discriminatory manner. A number of international

---

[307] In 1992, the CEDAW Committee adopted a general recommendation and comments on states' obligations under CEDAW that set forth the elements of potentially effective remedies to address the problem of violence against women as follows:

    a. Effective legal measures, including penal sanctions, civil remedies and compensatory provisions to protect women against all kinds of violence, including *inter alia* violence and abuse in the family, sexual assault and sexual harassment in the workplace;

    b. Preventive measures, including public information and education programmes to change attitudes concerning the roles and status of men and women;

    c. Protective measures, including refuges, counseling, rehabilitation and support services for women who are the victims of violence or who are at risk of violence.

Committee on the Elimination of All Forms of Violence Against Women, "Violence Against Women," General Recommendation no. 19 (eleventh session, 1992), U.N. Document CEDAW/C/1992/L.1/Add.15.

X. South Africa's Obligations Under International and National Law

treaties, to which the South African government has acceded, recognize education as a fundamental right.[308] Each treaty includes nondiscrimination language such that the right to education must be ensured for all children. Consistent with nondiscrimination provisions of international human rights treaties, when a state provides education for its children, it may not arbitrarily deny education to particular groups of children. According to international legal standards, no child should be denied an education on the basis of race, color, sex, language, religion, national or social origin, property or birth.

The right to education is enshrined in article 26 of the Universal Declaration of Human Rights, which provides that: "Everyone has the right to education. Education shall be free, at least in the elementary and fundamental stages. Elementary education shall be compulsory." The International Covenant on Economic, Social and Cultural Rights (ICESCR), which South Africa has signed, requires free and compulsory primary education and has a broad nondiscrimination clause.[309] Article 13(1) of the ICESCR states that: "The States Parties to the present Covenant recognize the right of everyone to education."[310]

The Convention on the Rights of the Child, article 28, guarantees "the right of the child to education" as a fundamental human right. The convention requires states to endeavor "with a view to achieving [the right to education] progressively and on the basis of equal opportunity" to provide free and compulsory primary education available to all. It calls upon states to make forms of secondary education available and accessible to every child, and to take

---

[308] Various regional treaties also establish education as a fundamental right. For instance, the African Charter on Human and Peoples' Rights guarantees a broad right to education in article 17 (1), which provides that "Every individual shall have the right to education." Article 17 of the charter provides further that the right to education must be guaranteed without distinction as to sex.

[309] Although the International Covenant on Civil and Political Rights (ICCPR), which South Africa has ratified, does not list primary education as a core civil and political right, article 24 of the ICCPR guarantees each child "the right to such measures of protection as are required by his status as a minor on the part of his family society and the State." This provision of article 24 has been interpreted to include education sufficient to enable each child to develop his or her capacities and enjoy civil and political rights as a measure of protection. U.N. Human Rights Committee, General Comment no. 17, para. 3. On the right to education in international law, see, generally, Manfred Nowak, "The Right to Education," in Asbjorn Eide et al. (eds.) *Economic, Social, and Cultural Rights* (1995), pp. 189-211.

[310] South Africa signed the ICESCR on October 3, 1994, but has not yet ratified the treaty.

measure to encourage regular attendance at schools and reduce dropout rates.[311] Similarly, CEDAW acknowledges the existence of a right to education and calls for states to dismantle barriers that block access to education for women.[312]

International law thus requires that a state providing education to its citizens must assure equal access to education for all its citizens. Women and girls must be able to enjoy education on equal terms with men and boys. In addition to requiring the provision of elementary education, the Universal Declaration of Human Rights and the ICESCR prohibit discrimination in all matters they address, including the provision of education. Article 2(2) of the ICESCR provides: "The States Parties to the present Covenant undertake to guarantee that the rights enunciated in the present Covenant will be exercised without discrimination of any kind as to race, colour, sex, language, religion, political or other opinion, national or social origin, property birth or other status." Article 3 focuses on women in particular: "The States Parties to the present Covenant undertake to ensure the equal rights of men and women to the enjoyment of all economic, social and cultural rights set forth in the present Covenant."

National Law

Consistent with international legal standards, South African constitutional law enshrines the right to bodily and psychological integrity and the right to life, and recognizes the inherent dignity of all human beings and the right to have that dignity respected and protected. The South African constitution prohibits unfair discrimination against anyone directly or indirectly on the basis of sex,

---

[311] South Africa ratified the CRC on December 15, 1995.
[312] Article 10 of CEDAW provides that state parties ensure equality of education between women and men at all levels from preschool to professional as follows:
> State Parties shall take all appropriate measures to eliminate discrimination against women in order to ensure the equal rights with men in the field of education and in particular to ensure, on a basis of equality of men and women:
> a. The same conditions for career and vocational guidance, for access to studies and for the achievement of diplomas in educational establishments of all categories in rural as well as in urban areas; this equality shall be ensured in preschool, general, technical, professional and higher technical education, as well as all types of vocational training;
> b. Access to the same curricula, the same examinations, teaching staff with qualifications of the same standard and school premises and equipment of the same quality;
> c. The elimination of any stereotyped concept of the roles of men and women at all levels and in all forms of education…in particular, by the revision of textbooks and school programmes and the adaptation of teaching methods;
> d. The same opportunities to benefit from scholarships and other study grants.

X. South Africa's Obligations Under International and National Law

gender, or pregnancy.[313] The constitution also guarantees the right to a basic education, including adult basic education.[314]

National legislation makes school attendance compulsory for South African children.[315] Pursuant to the South African Schools Act, "a public school must admit learners and serve their educational requirements without unfairly discriminating in any way." Because the government makes education compulsory for all, it cannot discriminate in the provision of public schooling.

The South African government is obligated to provide an education system that does not discriminate on the basis of sex pursuant to international human rights treaties it has ratified as well as national legislation it has promulgated. Failure to prevent and redress persistent gender-based violence in all its forms—from rape to sexual harassment—operates as a de facto discriminatory deprivation of the right to education for girl children in violation of international and national legal obligations.

The purpose of education, as enshrined in the Convention on the Rights of the Child, is to foster development of the child's personality, talent, and mental and physical abilities to their fullest potential to prepare him or her for responsible life in a free society, in the spirit of understanding, peace, tolerance, equality of the sexes, and friendship among all peoples.[316] Unchallenged gender-based violence in schools impedes the ability of all children to attain the educational objectives set forth in the convention. Where gender-based violence occurring in educational settings is not effectively halted and prosecuted, the enjoyment by girls of the fundamental human right to education on a basis of equality with others is impaired.

---

[313] Act No. 108 of 1996, Section 9.
[314] Ibid., Section 29.
[315] South African Schools Act No. 84 of 1996, Section 3(1) provides:
   Every parent must cause every learner for whom he or she is responsible to attend a school from the first school day of the year in which such learner reaches the age of seven years until the last school day of the year in which such learner reaches the age of 15 years or the ninth grade, whichever occurs first.
[316] Convention on the Rights of the Child, article 29.

XI. CONCLUSION

Acts of sexual violence and violence against girls at school remain unchallenged by school officials and exact a terrible cost to educational quality and equality in South Africa—in addition to violating girls' right to bodily integrity. A school environment where sexual violence and harassment is tolerated compromises the right of girl children to enjoy education on equal terms with boys—a lesson that is damaging to all children and at sharp variance with South Africa's constitution and its international legal obligations.

Quality education is predicated on all students being able to participate in education safely and without fear. The response of the education system to the issue of sexual violence and harassment goes to the heart of how a society responds to the challenge of creating gender equality. Children can best learn respect for human rights and gender equality where those principles are safeguarded and experienced in their own lives.

The South African education system is uniquely situated to play an important part in combating gender inequality. It is not only the curriculum that teaches children respect for human rights; the context in which learning takes place also informs the lesson. If the South African education system is ever to achieve nondiscriminatory education for all children, it must prioritize and place full political and financial support behind efforts to end gender violence in its schools. If the South African government is serious about its pledge to educational equality, the national and provincial education departments must coordinate to take immediate steps to address the violence girls face in school by fulfilling its responsibility to prohibit and protect girls against such abuses. Going forward, schools need to find ways to heal, rehabilitate, and build a culture of respect for girls and to address the trauma created by the violent crime experienced by so many children.

The government is already taking some important steps to achieve this vision, in the face of great challenges created by the legacy of apartheid and the resource limitations of the present. Human Rights Watch hopes that this report will assist in further strengthening those efforts. We also hope that this analysis of the problem of sexual violence in South African schools and the government response to that violence can inform debates on similar issues elsewhere in the world. Girls everywhere face gender-based violence in schools that impedes equal access to education. Stronger efforts to address such violence are essential to achieving the aim, stated by the World Education Forum in the 2000 Dakar Framework for Action, of gender equality in education by 2015 with full and equal access to and achievement in education for girls.

ACKNOWLEDGEMENTS

This report was written by Erika George, Alan Finberg fellow with the Academic Freedom Program of Human Rights Watch, based on research conducted in South Africa from late March to early April 2000 by the author and Yodon Thonden, counsel to the Children's Rights Division. It was edited by Joe Saunders, former Director of the Academic Freedom Program, Bronwen Manby of the Africa Division, and Michael McClintock, Deputy Program Director. LaShawn Jefferson, Deputy Director of the Women's Rights Division, and Michael Bochenek and Joanne Csete of the Children's Rights Division provided valuable insights and helpful comments. James Ross of the Human Rights Watch legal and policy office provided legal review. Production assistance was provided by Jonathan Horowitz.

Many people provided us with helpful information, guidance, and assistance in South Africa. Our special thanks go to Joan van Niekerk, founder and executive director of Childline, for her generous assistance in facilitating our research. We are also especially grateful for the assistance of Charlene Smith of the *Mail and Guardian*. We also wish to thank Lynn Cawood, Colin AJ Collett van Rooyen, Michael Sikhakhane, Helen Gumede, Cheryl Jarman, Ravni Chetty, Kimberley Porteus, Joy Pelo, Sthokozo Nxumalo, Betty George, Nan Stein, Susan Fineran, Claudia Mitchell, Margaret Roper, Thuli Shongwe, Sue Goldstone, Harriet Perlman, Eric Richardson, Janet Walsh, Zetu Makamandela, Cathy Albertyn, Marietjie Myberg, Ruta van NieKerk, and Nicolette Moodie.

Human Rights Watch thanks Resources Aimed at the Prevention of Child Abuse and Neglect in Cape Town and all the Childline offices in Gauteng, KwaZulu-Natal, and the Western Cape. We also owe a special debt of gratitude to the Crime Reduction in Schools Project in KwaZulu-Natal and the Safe Schools Project in the Western Cape. We are grateful to the many school officials who allowed us to interview them and their students.

Most especially, we wish to express our deep appreciation to the many courageous girls who spoke with us and thank them and their families for sharing their stories.

Support for this project came in part from the Ford Foundation.

APPENDICES

Appendix A:
Human Rights Watch Report Recommendations (1997) and (1995)

Violence Against Women and the Medico-Legal System (1997)

In addition to the general recommendations in its 1995 report, Violence Against Women in South Africa: The State Response to Domestic Violence and Rape, Human Rights Watch makes the following recommendations to the South African government specifically relating to the medico-legal system and its response to violence against women. Some of these recommendations are already being implemented in some provinces, others have received less attention. We believe that all are necessary.

General Recommendations:

- Women who have been sexually assaulted and report to a police station should be taken by the police to be examined by a specialist medico-legal practitioner as soon as possible, to ensure that forensic evidence is not lost and to allow the complainant to wash herself and change as soon as possible. There is no need for a full statement to be taken by the police at the time of initial reporting.

- Women who have been sexually assaulted and report to a public health facility should wherever possible be examined for medico-legal purposes at that facility, if necessary after calling a specialist from elsewhere to carry out the examination. The woman should be informed of her right to lay a charge and, with her consent, police should be called to the facility for the crime to be reported.

- Following medico-legal examination, government policy should pay greater attention to the need for women to receive appropriate treatment for injuries, infections, or other related trauma. Women should be informed in writing and orally in their own language (if possible), or in a language they understand, about governmental and nongovernmental support services available and referred for counseling. Special care should be taken to ensure that a woman who decides to lay a charge against her assailant and who therefore requires a medico-legal examination (a purely diagnostic procedure) is not effectively deterred or prevented from also obtaining treatment for her injuries.

- Private practitioners who treat women who have been sexually assaulted should have sufficient training and information at their disposal to be able to advise their patients of the desirability of a medico-legal examination by a specialist and refer them to the nearest facility where that is possible.

- Government departments should ensure through training and distribution of information that all those who have contact with victims of sexual assault in an official capacity, whether in the health or criminal justice system, are able to refer them to appropriate governmental and nongovernmental support services and to inform them of their rights.

- Efforts should be made to increase the number of women practicing in the medico-legal field and to ensure that a woman who has been assaulted is examined by other women where possible, or that another woman health worker is present while the examination is conducted.

- In developing policy initiatives, the problems faced by women and children and the solutions suggested should be disaggregated and addressed as separate issues.

District surgeons/medico-legal practitioners:

- In reforming district surgeon services, attention should be paid to the urgent need to ensure adequate expertise in medico-legal matters among those doctors providing medico-legal services. Although the integration of medico-legal services with general primary health care responsibilities would be a welcome step toward making those services more accessible, an examination carried out by an inexperienced and untrained doctor may be useless. As accessibility improves, every effort must be made to ensure that quality is maintained by requiring thorough and appropriate training for all medico-legal practitioners.

- Training programs should be developed for those appointed to carry out medico-legal work, both as a requirement before appointment and as annual in-service training. These programs should include information on the technical aspects of medico-legal practice and education on the psychological impact of sexual assault on the victim.

- Manuals should be developed for newly appointed district surgeons (or district medical officers, as they are now to be known) which outline the relevant laws for their work, review the necessary specialized medical information (for example, ways of determining the time of injury), and provide detailed descriptions of injuries specific to sexual assault in both adult and child victims.

- Standardized protocols for the examination and treatment of survivors of rape and sexual assault and the collection of biological samples should be developed and distributed to all those engaged in medico-legal work.

- Specialized curricula in clinical forensic medicine for medical students should be developed by the universities offering medical training and made compulsory for all medical students, with practical expertise in a medico-legal clinic a requirement of such courses; a qualification in clinical forensic medicine, similar to that for forensic pathologists, should also be developed and made available to those doctors who wish to specialize in this area of work.

- Specialized curricula in clinical forensic medicine for nurses should be developed, and a qualification in clinical forensic practice made available to nurses who wish to specialize in this area. The possibility of specialized nurses carrying out medico-legal examinations should be investigated.

- The Medical Association of South Africa, which publishes a journal of continuing medical education, should arrange for a special edition of this publication dealing with medico-legal aspects of violence against women.

Police:

- Police investigating officers handling sexual assault and rape cases should specialize in such investigations and be trained in the issues surrounding gender violence and the use of medical and other forensic evidence.

The courts:

- Specialized curricula in clinical forensic medicine for law students should be developed and successful completion of such a course made compulsory for lawyers applying to become prosecutors or magistrates.

- Justice College, in Pretoria, where prosecutors and magistrates are trained, should include courses on the use of medical evidence within its syllabi.

- As is already the trend, each regional magistrates court should identify specialized prosecutors to handle cases of sexual abuse and rape, who should receive additional training in the issues surrounding such violence.

- Where appropriate, the use of doctors as lay assessors to sit with magistrates to judge sexual assault cases should be encouraged.

- The Department of Justice should make available specialized training in medico-legal vocabulary to court interpreters.

- Legislation should be introduced to abolish the use of the "cautionary rule" in rape cases, which requires courts to exercise additional care in assessing the credibility of a rape survivor. The cautionary rule in rape cases places a particular premium on corroborative evidence if a woman is to win her case.

The collection and analysis of medico-legal evidence:

- The J88 form, used to record the findings of a medico-legal examination, should be redesigned along the lines set out in the body of this report.

- The Pretoria forensic biology laboratory, and forensic services in general, should be taken out of control of the police and placed under the Department of Health, with an independent status, similar for example to that of the attorneys general.

Collection and dissemination of information on violence against women:

- All health facilities should have information on display and available to be taken away on the medico-legal and other services available to women who have been subjected to sexual assault or domestic violence.

- A national directory of governmental and nongovernmental services available to women should be developed, and information should be distributed to police stations and magistrates courts, as well as to district surgeons, hospitals and other health care facilities about locally available referral services for women who have been assaulted.

- In designing data collection models, the specific issues of violence against women should be addressed (for example, the means of collecting statistics from the health services on both rape and domestic violence, or the possibility of making rape a reportable occurrence as child abuse already is).

Violence Against Women in South Africa (1995)

Recommendations to the Government of South Africa:

Legal Reform:

International Law:

- While Human Rights Watch is encouraged by the South African government's efforts to sign Convention on the Elimination of All Forms of Discrimination against Women, it urges the government to formally ratify CEDAW without further delay.

Domestic Violence:

- The 1993 Prevention of Family Violence Act should be expanded (1) to include protection for individuals who are abused by a partner with whom they have never lived and lesbian and gay couples and (2) to extend jurisdiction over abuse cases to ensure that women can be protected wherever they are in South Africa when the abuse occurs.

Appendix: A

- The Department of Justice should issue guidelines for magistrates in order to clarify the types of abuse which would qualify for an interdict (a form of restraining order) under the Prevention of Family Violence Act. These guidelines should expressly include both verbal and emotional abuse, in addition to physical abuse.

- Delays in payments to agents—the sheriffs—responsible for delivering court orders prohibiting abuse should never be considered a justification for failing immediately to deliver interdicts that have been issued as emergency remedies to domestic violence.

- Legal provisions must be introduced to protect counseling service workers who advise abused women from violence or threats of violence directed against them by their clients' abusive partners.

- Without diminishing protection to domestically-abused women, policymakers must address the concern that interdicts granted under the Prevention of Family Violence Act may violate the *audi alteram partem* rule(which allows both sides to present their cases before courts) because such interdicts are issued without a hearing and are for unspecified durations. One possibility might be to create a temporary interdict order which can be made final after a hearing.

- Guidelines must be adopted by the police and prosecution service on arrest and prosecution policy so that domestic violence cases are accorded the full attention of the criminal justice system. Family violence cases must not be treated as "private problems" and therefore not suitable for intervention by the criminal justice system. Appropriate sentencing policies must be developed, including compulsory attendance at programs designed for abusive partners.

- Prosecutors must be trained to deal with domestic violence cases in accord with clear guidelines. While prosecutional discretion must be safeguarded, prosecutors should be instructed to refrain from dropping cases of domestic abuse and to argue for strict bail conditions to be imposed where there is a history of violent assault.

Rape:

- It should be recognized in law that this crime can be committed by men or women against men or women. The definition of rape should be broadened to include anal and oral penetration as well as penetration by foreign objects such as sticks, bottles, or knives. The definition should focus on coercion by the perpetrator rather than lack of consent by the victim.

- Legislation should be introduced to abolish the use of the cautionary rule, which permits courts to exercise an excessive level of discretion in deciding whether or not to credit the testimony of women who allege they have been raped, in cases of rape or sexual assault, on the grounds that it discriminates against women on the basis of sex.

- Guidelines on sentencing for rape should be adopted by the Department of Justice and circulated to all judges. At the moment, rape sentences are wide-ranging and appear to be related more to the judge's views on rape than to any consistent application of established standards.

- Judges, magistrates, and prosecutors should receive mandatory training on rape and domestic violence and in the use of medico-legal evidence.

Improved Police Services:
The police appear to be a major impediment to effective action in addressing violence against women.

- A standard course of training on domestic violence, rape, and sexual assault should be completed by new recruits and by serving officers. The government should commission individuals and institutions with expertise in this area to develop such a program and should work together with the relevant government departments to effect its implementation on a national scale. Law enforcement personnel should be trained in procedures and enforcement of the Prevention of Family Violence Act and about the social and psychological context in which domestic violence occurs.

- Police are obligated to ensure protection and equal enforcement of the law in domestic abuse cases. Police must be trained to eliminate gender, class and race bias in their responses to such abuse and to realize that domestic violence is not to be excused, tolerated or condoned. Standardized arrest policies should be considered for domestic violence cases.

- Police who are involved in investigating rape cases should receive proper training in forensic skills and in the importance of medical information.

- Police must provide prompt protection to women by diligently enforcing court orders that prohibit abuse and reduce the abuser's access to the victim. Police stations must make it a priority to respond speedily to a woman's urgent call in cases of domestic violence.

- The government should create an independent mechanism to monitor and oversee police treatment of women victims of violence. This body should be empowered to hear complaints and to take steps to sanction police officers who do not act professionally, including cases in which the abused woman is a partner of a police officer.

The Medico-Legal System:

- Provincial authorities should review government health services directly responsible for the examination and treatment of rape survivors to ensure the most responsive, effective, and accessible delivery of service.

- The Department of Health should establish standardized procedures and services to ensure that all district surgeons are appropriately trained in the treatment of rape and domestic violence survivors. The treatment should be expanded from the collection of medical evidence to the provision of basic medical treatment. This after-care should include, at a minimum, medical treatment, emotional support and referral to the nearest counseling service. District surgeons should be required to provide rape survivors with information about additional existing services in the area.

- More district surgeons should be appointed in the rural areas.

- Rape reporting centers, modeled on the Hillbrow Medico-Legal Clinic, should be established as widely as possible, and in particular in townships. Such facilities must be staffed by trained police and medical personnel to allow victims to report cases of rape or battery, undergo medical examination, and receive appropriate treatment and counseling.

- Abortion laws which protect the right for rape victims to have access to abortion should be upheld without discrimination.

Inter-Departmental Coordination:
The effectiveness of the law depends on cooperation and coordination among implementing law enforcement, judicial and social service agencies.

- A national multi-disciplinary task-force on violence against women should be created to improve social, medical and legal procedures for women affected by violence. It should include, at a minimum, representatives from the Departments of Justice, Safety and Security, Health and Welfare. Liaison officers in each of the relevant departments at the state and provincial levels should be authorized to communicate and initiate changes within their department in coordination with the other departments and in consultation with nongovernmental organizations. One function would be to expedite the creation of local units, like the Hillbrow Medico-Legal Clinic, to attend to the needs of abused and raped women.

- Regional forums, similar to the Johannesburg rape forum, should be established in each province with government and nongovernmental organizations on it. Government representatives should include district surgeons, police, and the Department of Justice.

- In each province, the government should form a working group in which governmental and nongovernmental organizations meet on a regular basis in order to improve the government's response to and services for domestic violence and rape victims.

- The government should help fund the creation of legal assistance programs, accessible and affordable shelters, as well as counseling services for abused women.

Documentation of Violence against Women:
Efforts to improve the South African government's response to domestic abuse and rape would be greatly enhanced by the availability

of reliable national data detailing the nature and degree of the violence. At the moment, police do not distinguish cases of domestic violence from other assaults, while national statistics regarding rape are not comprehensively compiled.

- We urge the South African government to improve the collection of data concerning crimes of violence against women. We recommend that the government first conduct a review of all existing statistical information. Such a review should include, at a minimum, the incidence of such violence, the identity of the parties, rates of prosecution and nature of punishment. The collection and reporting of statistics must also be improved, specifically to distinguish domestic violence cases from other assaults. Sufficient details should be recorded to create profiles of victims and perpetrators, including their racial and class status, so that intervention to stop or remedy abuse can be most effectively crafted. Efforts must be made to survey the extent of unreported violence against women.

- Studies of the nature and extent of violence against women should be carried out or funded by the government in close cooperation with nongovernmental organizations active in this field.

Appendix B:
South African Student Essays and Letters on Crime and Violence

The following testimonials were written in English as class exercises by students from KwaZulu-Natal schools participating in the Crime Reduction in Schools Program. The CRISP Program is described in detail in the report. These and other student essays are on file with CRISP at the University of Natal, Durban. In April 2000, Human Rights Watch visited the schools participating in CRISP. Selected essays and letters are attached.

March 1999
This is about raping and
stealing somboddiy Trid to
rap me in the girls' ToiLtls
Then He Lrid to Kach me
With a rope then I ran away

My name is _____ and I am in grade 7 K at _____ School. My full address is _____. I live with my mom and dad. Every morning at half past seven I walk to school. It is not so bad walking to school because I live so close.

I remember a couple of weeks ago I read about a 14 year old girl who had been raped by seven men, and I also remember how scared I felt because I am almost the same age as her and what if that had been me. Before I read the story I used to walk to the shop with out any worry, but now I am terrified to walk alone so I either go to the shop with my friends or my parents.

After that my parents had decided that they want to move to Austrailia because of the high crime rate in South Africa, I also want to move because would like to be able to walk down the road with out the fear of being kidnapped or raped. I would like to be able to grow up with out the fear and violence that crime causes. sometimes I just cry because I get so scared that something might happen to me or my family. I am not even allowed to go to the beach with my friends. I don't blame my parents for this I blame the crime.

Appendix: B

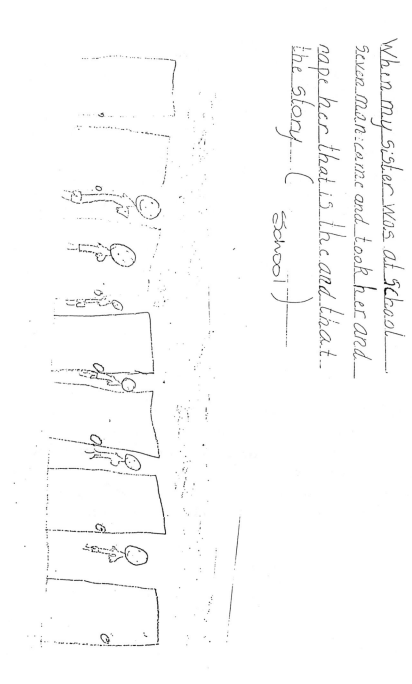

When my sister was at school seven man came and took her and rape her that is the and that the story — (school)

A chat with myself!

Im a young girl named _____ who is in Grade 7 _____ and I school at _____ Primary school. At _____ the moment I am living in _____ with my aunt and her family. I do not live with my parents because they live far away and they wanted me to live in the surburb with my aunt so I can school at schools which have good facilities and most important a good education. The problem that I have is I am not happy where I am living because if bad things happen to me I tell my aunt and her eldest daughter but they laugh at me and ignore me, so I can not live with people whom I hardly even talk to. I feel that as a young girl who is growing needs to be close to her mother so she can talk "woman" things. Another reason is there are too many strangers and when I come from school they falow me. They are always up to something but I see before they make a move.

Appendix: B

A chat with myself...

My name is _____ I'm in grade seven
Mrs. _____ at _____ Primary School.
I live at _____ I live with both
my parents and are married. I have
_____ brothers _____ which are
younger than me.
I come and go to school by car which
is safe for me because if I take a bus
I have to walk a long distance and it
puts my life at risk. The car I come
with take me and leaves me at the
gate of my house.

Dear Reader

One afternoon when I was 60 in Primary School my sister came to fetch me at 4 ou to where my mother worked in

My sister had been wearing her short jean shorts and a top. She had been carring my bag. We walked talking and laughing together.

We walked until we met 2 guys in the middle of the way they asked us for the way to Primary School. I reply replied to them saying "just walk all the through this bush and the turn to your right twice. They said Thank you

One of them said to my sister that she looked beautiful. She said Thanks. One guy grabed her and said I like you. They both grabed her pushed her on the floor I escaped/runned away from them

My sister told me to run away instead I hid I in the bushes and crying quietly my heart was beating hard I saw those "bastereds" rape my sisters, they tore her clothes.

I got so angry that I ran as fast as I could towards my mothers place of work my school uniform was wet with tears. I was angry disappointed of myself because I was powerless I couldn't do anything.

After a few months my sister was carring a child she didn't know who the father was. She was terrified.

But luckily she got through it.

Name:
Age: 11 years old   – Grade 6
Teacher: Mr
Home address:
How I get to school: I travel by bus
Who I live with: My mother and father and my younger sister.

Crime I have seen:

My sister, a friend of mine and I were coming home from school when we saw a man hitting a teenage girl. Everyone walked past them and didn't try to stop. We certainly couldn't. He was dragging her, banging her head against the wall and pulling her hair. She was crying and I don't blame her for doing so. We quickly walked past them, we ~~wal~~ walked far enough to still see them. We stopped again and watched, I don't know why I did. After a while we carried on walking back home. I just couldn't sleep well that night.

Appendix C:
South African Council for Educators Code of Conduct

CODE OF CONDUCT

DEFINITIONS

1. In this code, unless the context indicates otherwise:

- **"educator"** means any person who teaches, educates or trains other persons or provides professional therapy at any school, technical college or college of education or assists in rendering professional services or performs education management services or educational auxiliary services provided by or in a department of education, (and whose employment is regulated by the Educators' Employment Act, 1994); and any other person registered with the Council;

- **"learner"** means a pupil or a student who is taught or trained by an educator as defined above;

- **"parent"** means -

  (a) the parent or guardian of a learner;

  (b) the person legally entitled to custody of a learner; or

  (c) the person who undertakes to fulfil the obligations of a person referred to in paragraphs (a) and (b) towards the learner's education at school.

PREAMBLE

2. The educators who are registered with the South African Council for Educators -

   2.1 acknowledge the noble calling of their profession to educate and train the learners of our country;

   2.2 acknowledge that the attitude, dedication, self-discipline, ideals, training and conduct of the teaching profession determine the quality of education in this country;

   2.3 acknowledge, uphold and promote basic human rights, as embodied in the Constitution of South Africa;

   2.4 commit themselves to do all within their power, in the exercising of their professional duties, to act in accordance with the ideals of their profession, as expressed in this code; and

   2.5 act in a proper and becoming way such that their behaviour does not bring the teaching profession into disrepute.

CONDUCT: THE EDUCATOR AND THE LEARNER

3. An educator -

   3.1 respects the dignity, beliefs and constitutional rights of learners and in particular children, which includes the right to privacy and confidentiality;

   3.2 acknowledges the uniqueness, individuality, and specific needs of each learner, guiding and encouraging each to realise his or her potentialities;

   3.3 strives to enable learners to develop a set of values consistent with those upheld in the Bill of Rights as contained in the Constitution of South Africa;

   3.4 exercises authority with compassion;

   3.5 avoids any form of humiliation, and refrains from any form of child abuse, physical or psychological;

   3.6 promotes gender equality and refrains from any form of sexual relationship with learners or sexual harassment (physical or otherwise) of learners;

   3.7 uses appropriate language and behaviour in his or her interaction with learners, and acts in such a way as to elicit respect from the learners;

   3.8 takes reasonable steps to ensure the safety of the learner;

   3.9 does not abuse the position he or she holds for financial, political or personal gain;

Appendix: C

3.10 is not negligent or indolent in the performance of his or her professional duties;

3.11 recognises, where appropriate, learners as partners in education.

CONDUCT: THE EDUCATOR AND THE PARENT

An educator, where appropriate -

4.1 recognises the parents as partners in education, and promotes a harmonious relationship with them;

4.2 does what is practically possible to keep parents adequately and timeously informed about the well-being and progress of the learner.

CONDUCT: THE EDUCATOR AND THE COMMUNITY

An educator recognises that an educational institution serves the community, and therefore acknowledges that there will be differing customs, codes and beliefs in the community.

CONDUCT: THE EDUCATOR AND HIS OR HER COLLEAGUES

An educator -

6.1 refrains from undermining the status and authority of his or her colleagues;

6.2 promotes gender equality and refrains from sexual harassment (physical or otherwise) of his or her colleagues;

6.3 respects the various responsibilities assigned to colleagues and the authority that arises therefrom, to ensure the smooth running of the educational institution;

6.4 uses proper procedures to address issues of professional incompetence or misbehaviour.

CONDUCT: THE EDUCATOR AND THE PROFESSION

7. An educator -

7.1 acknowledges that the exercising of his or her professional duties occurs within a context requiring co-operation with and support of colleagues, and therefore behaves in such a way as to enhance the dignity and status of the profession;

7.2 keeps abreast of educational trends and developments;

7.3 promotes the ongoing development of teaching as a profession;

7.4 accepts that he or she has a professional obligation towards the education and induction into the profession of new members of the teaching profession.

CONDUCT: THE EDUCATOR AND HIS OR HER EMPLOYER

8. An educator -

8.1 recognises the employer as a partner in education;

8.2 acknowledges that certain responsibilities and authorities are vested in the employer through legislation, and serves his or her employer to the best of his or her ability;

8.3 refrains from discussing confidential and official matters with unauthorised persons.

CONDUCT: THE EDUCATOR AND THE COUNCIL

9. An educator -

9.1 co-operates with the South African Council for Educators to the best of his or her ability;

9.2 accepts and complies with the Disciplinary Powers and Procedures of the South African Council for Educators.

Appendix D:
Dakar World Education for All Forum Framework Document

The Dakar Framework for Action

Education For All:
Meeting Our Collective Commitments

Text adopted by
the World Education Forum
Dakar, Senegal, 26-28 April 2000

1. Meeting in Dakar, Senegal, in April 2000, we, the participants in the World Education Forum, commit ourselves to the achievement of education for all (EFA) goals and targets for every citizen and for every society.

2. The Dakar Framework is a collective commitment to action. Governments have an obligation to ensure that EFA goals and targets are reached and sustained. This is a responsibility that will be met most effectively through broad-based partnerships within countries, supported by cooperation with regional and international agencies and institutions.

3. We re-affirm the vision of the World Declaration on Education for All (Jomtien 1990), supported by the Universal Declaration of Human Rights and the Convention on the Rights of the Child, that all children, young people and adults have the human right to benefit from an education that will meet their basic learning needs in the best and fullest sense of the term, an education that includes learning to know, to do, to live together and to be. It is an education geared to tapping each individual's talents and potential, and developing learners' personalities, so that they can improve their lives and transform their societies.

4. We welcome the commitments made by the international community to basic education throughout the 1990s, notably at the World Summit for Children (1990), the Conference on Environment and Development (1992), the World Conference on Human Rights (1993), the World Conference on Special Needs Education: Access and Quality (1994), the International Conference on Population and Development (1994), the World Summit for Social Development (1995), the Fourth World Conference on Women (1995), the Mid-Term Meeting of the International Consultative Forum on Education for All (1996), the Fifth International Conference on Adult Education (1997), and the International Conference on Child Labour (1997). The challenge now is to deliver on these commitments.

5. The EFA 2000 Assessment demonstrates that there has been significant progress in many countries. But it is unacceptable in the year 2000 that more than 113 million children have no access to primary education, 880 million adults are illiterate, gender discrimination continues to permeate education systems, and the quality of learning and the acquisition of human values and skills fall far short of the aspirations and

needs of individuals and societies. Youth and adults are denied access to the skills and knowledge necessary for gainful employment and full participation in their societies. Without accelerated progress towards education for all, national and internationally agreed targets for poverty reduction will be missed, and inequalities between countries and within societies will widen.

6. Education is a fundamental human right. It is the key to sustainable development and peace and stability within and among countries, and thus an indispensable means for effective participation in the societies and economies of the twenty-first century, which are affected by rapid globalization. Achieving EFA goals should be postponed no longer. The basic learning needs of all can and must be met as a matter of urgency

7. We hereby collectively commit ourselves to the attainment of the following goals:

(i) expanding and improving comprehensive early childhood care and education, especially for the most vulnerable and disadvantaged children;

(ii) ensuring that by 2015 all children, particularly girls, children in difficult circumstances and those belonging to ethnic minorities, have access to and complete free and compulsory primary education of good quality;

(iii) ensuring that the learning needs of all young people and adults are met through equitable access to appropriate learning and life skills programmes;

(iv) achieving a 50 per cent improvement in levels of adult literacy by 2015, especially for women, and equitable access to basic and continuing education for all adults;

(v) eliminating gender disparities in primary and secondary education by 2005, and achieving gender equality in education by 2015, with a focus on ensuring girls' full and equal access to and achievement in basic education of good quality;

(vi) improving all aspects of the quality of education and ensuring excellence of all so that recognized and measurable learning outcomes are achieved by all, especially in literacy, numeracy and essential life skills.

8. To achieve these goals, we the governments, organizations, agencies, groups and associations represented at the World Education Forum pledge ourselves to:

(i) mobilize strong national and international political commitment for education for all, develop national action plans and enhance significantly investment in basic education;

(ii) promote EFA policies within a sustainable and well-integrated sector framework clearly linked to poverty elimination and development strategies;

(iii) ensure the engagement and participation of civil society in the formulation, implementation and monitoring of strategies for educational development;

(iv) develop responsive, participatory and accountable systems of educational governance and management;

(v) meet the needs of education systems affected by conflict, national calamities and instability and conduct educational programmes in ways that promote mutual understanding, peace and tolerance, and help to prevent violence and conflict;

(vi) implement integrated strategies for gender equality in education which recognize the need for changes in attitudes, values and practices;

(vii) implement as a matter of urgency education programmes and actions to combat the HIV/AIDS pandemic;

(viii) create safe, healthy, inclusive and equitably resourced educational environments conducive to excellence in learning with clearly defined levels of achievement for all;

(ix) enhance the status, morale and professionalism of teachers;

(x) harness new information and communication technologies to help achieve EFA goals;

(xi) systematically monitor progress towards EFA goals and strategies at the national, regional and international levels; and

(xii) build on existing mechanisms to accelerate progress towards education for all.

9. Drawing on the evidence accumulated during the national and regional EFA assessments, and building on existing national sector strategies, all States will be requested to develop or strengthen existing national plans of action by 2002 at the latest. These plans should be integrated into a wider poverty reduction and development framework, and should be developed through more transparent and democratic processes, involving stakeholders, especially peoples' representatives, community leaders, parents, learners, non-governmental organizations (NGOs) and civil society. The plans will address problems associated with the chronic under-financing of basic education by establishing budget priorities that reflect a commitment to achieving EFA goals and targets at the earliest possible date, and no later than 2015. They will also set out clear strategies for overcoming the special problems facing those currently excluded from educational opportunities, with a clear commitment to girls' education and gender equity. The plans will give substance and form to the goals and strategies set out in this Framework, and to the commitments made during a succession of international conferences in the 1990s. Regional activities to support national strategies will be based on strengthened regional and subregional organizations, networks and initiatives.

* 10. Political will and stronger national leadership are needed for the effective and successful implementation of national plans in each of the countries concerned. However, political will must be underpinned by resources. The international community acknowledges that many countries currently lack the resources to achieve education for all within an acceptable time-frame. New financial resources, preferably in the form of grants and concessional assistance, must therefore be mobilized by bilateral and multilateral funding agencies, including the World Bank and regional development banks, and the private sector. We affirm that no countries seriously committed to education for all will be thwarted in their achievement of this goal by a lack of resources.

* 11. The international community will deliver on this collective commitment by launching with immediate effect a global initiative aimed at developing the strategies and mobilizing the resources needed to provide effective support to national efforts. Options to be considered under this initiative will include:

(i) increasing external finance for education, in particular basic education;

Appendix: D

(ii) ensuring greater predictability in the flow of external assistance;

(iii) facilitating more effective donor coordination;

(iv) strengthening sector-wide approaches;

(v) providing earlier, more extensive and broader debt relief and/or debt cancellation for poverty reduction, with a strong commitment to basic education; and

(vi) undertaking more effective and regular monitoring of progress towards EFA goals and targets, including periodic assessments.

* 12. There is already evidence from many countries of what can be achieved through strong national strategies supported by effective development cooperation. Progress under these strategies could - and must - be accelerated through increased international support. At the same time, countries with less developed strategies - including countries in transition, countries affected by conflict, and post-crisis countries - must be given the support they need to achieve more rapid progress towards education for all.

* 13. We will strengthen accountable international and regional mechanisms to give clear expression to these commitments and to ensure that the Dakar Framework for Action is on the agenda of every international and regional organization, every national legislature and every local decision-making forum.

* 14. The EFA 2000 Assessment highlights that the challenge of education for all is greatest in sub-Saharan Africa, in South Asia, and in the least developed countries. Accordingly, while no country in need should be denied international assistance, priority should be given to these regions and countries. Countries in conflict or undergoing reconstruction should also be given special attention in building up their education systems to meet the needs of all learners.

Build on existing mechanisms to accelerate progress towards EFA

* 15. Implementation of the preceding goals and strategies will require national, regional and international mechanisms to be galvanized immediately. To be most effective these mechanisms will be participatory and, wherever possible, build on what already exists. They will include representatives of all stakeholders and partners and they will operate in transparent and accountable ways. They will respond comprehensively to the word and spirit of the Jomtien Declaration and this Dakar Framework for Action. The functions of these mechanisms will include, to varying degrees, advocacy, resource mobilization, monitoring, and EFA knowledge generation and sharing.

* 16. The heart of EFA activity lies at the country level. National EFA Forums will be strengthened or established to support the achievement of EFA. All relevant ministries and national civil society organizations will be systematically represented in these Forums. They should be transparent and democratic and should constitute a framework for implementation at subnational levels. Countries will prepare comprehensive National EFA Plans by 2002 at the latest. For those countries with significant challenges, such as complex crises or natural disasters, special technical support will be provided by the international community. Each National EFA Plan will:

(i) be developed by government leadership in direct and systematic consultation with national civil society;

(ii) attract co-ordinated support of all development partners;

(iii) specify reforms addressing the six EFA goals;

(iv) establish a sustainable financial framework;

(v) be time-bound and action-oriented;

(vi) include mid-term performance indicators; and

(vii) achieve a synergy of all human development efforts, through its inclusion within the national development planning framework and process.

17. Where these processes and a credible plan are in place, partner members of the international community undertake to work in a consistent, co-ordinated and coherent manner. Each partner will contribute according to its comparative advantage in support of the National EFA Plans to ensure that resource gaps are filled.

18. Regional activities to support national efforts will be based on existing regional and subregional organizations, networks and initiatives, augmented where necessary. Regions and subregions will decide on a lead EFA network that will become the Regional or Subregional Forum with an explicit EFA mandate. Systematic involvement of, and co-ordination with, all relevant civil society and other regional and subregional organizations are essential. These Regional and Subregional EFA Forums will be linked organically with, and be accountable to, National EFA Forums. Their functions will be: co-ordination with all relevant networks; setting and monitoring regional/subregional targets; advocacy; policy dialogue; the promotion of partnerships and technical cooperation; the sharing of best practices and lessons learned; monitoring and reporting for accountability; and promoting resource mobilization. Regional and international support will be available to strengthen Regional and Subregional Forums and relevant EFA capacities, especially within Africa and South Asia.

19. UNESCO will continue its mandated role in co-ordinating EFA partners and maintaining their collaborative momentum. In line with this, UNESCO's Director-General will convene annually a high-level, small and flexible group. It will serve as a lever for political commitment and technical and financial resource mobilization. Informed by a monitoring report from the UNESCO International Institute for Educational Planning (IIEP), the UNESCO International Bureau of Education (IBE), the UNESCO Institute for Education (UIE) and, in particular, the UNESCO Institute of Statistics, and inputs from Regional and Subregional EFA Forums, it will also be an opportunity to hold the global community to account for commitments made in Dakar. It will be composed of highest-level leaders from governments and civil society of developing and developed countries, and from development agencies.

20. UNESCO will serve as the Secretariat. It will refocus its education programme in order to place the outcomes and priorities of Dakar at the heart of its work. This will involve working groups on each of the six goals adopted at Dakar. This Secretariat will work closely with other organizations and may include staff seconded from them.

21. Achieving Education for All will require additional financial support by countries and increased development assistance and debt relief for education by bilateral and multilateral donors, estimated to cost in the order of $8 billion a year. It is therefore essential that new, concrete financial commitments be made by national governments and also by bilateral and multilateral donors including the World Bank and the regional development banks, by civil society and by foundations.

28 April 2000 Dakar, Senegal